"This book is an informative, well researched and evidence-ba: wishing to incorporate the power of collage into their appr experienced it in action, Andréa Watts' innovative, considered ar second to none. It speaks to Andréa's generosity that she has be and codify the process for all within the pages of this great read. .... .pp.oach and wisdom will help to transform your approach with working with clients, helping you and them to reach full potential."

Jenny Garrett, OBE, Award-Winning Career Coach,
Leadership Trainer, Speaker & Author

"CCT offers coaches a new approach for fostering creativity within coaching sessions. Drawing on art therapy and the potential to explore both the conscious and unconscious representations we hold as individuals, the technique can be a powerful addition to unleashing the creative potential within clients through collage, story and wider art-based methods."

Jonathan Passmore, Director Henley Centre for Coaching,
Henley Business School

"A must read for coaches looking to engage in more creative techniques.

Andréa captures the essence of art-based methods and their impact on the coaching process, whilst drawing on personal experience, client feedback, and a wealth of scientific evidence.

The chapter of storytelling really gets to the crux of why collage is such a powerful tool in a coach's toolkit. Andréa highlights that *'By circumnavigating external influences, editing and fact-checking, their collage represents an honest, outer expression of their internal processing and the resulting sense of self'* – and in using images, as is explained in the chapter 'Coaching With the Unconscious', gets the client out of their usual mode of thinking to enable a deeper insight into their unconscious.

For me, the best thing about the way this book is written is that although it is not designed to be a *guide* as to how to integrate collage into coaching, in explaining the process and underlying science, Andréa also shares so much of her own expertise and client's experiences with the CCT, so that you get a real feel for how this would work in your own coaching practice."

Lynsey Mahmood, Lecturer in Organisational Psychology,
City, University of London

Collage as a Creative Coaching Tool

Collage as a Creative Coaching Tool is a stimulating and informative resource introducing the Collage Coaching Technique™. This three-stage creative process unlocks unconscious thinking, enabling profound psychological insight through a deeper and faster exploration of emotions and behaviours. Equipped with this awareness, clients are empowered to create meaningful and sustainable change.

Emphasis is on the qualities inherent in collage creation that allow clients to reconstruct their internal narrative and move forward purposefully and effectively. Essentially, by disassembling, disrupting, questioning, reassembling, and visualising their thoughts and emotions externally. Case studies, client reflections, and Andréa's experiences feature throughout, illustrating and enriching the theory. The content includes detailed guidance on creating a safe space for coaching creatively, applying Clean Language, coaching with collage online, and engaging groups in arts-based coaching. Through this comprehensive resource, the case for integrating collage in coaching and psychology is irrefutable.

It is inspirational and essential reading for anyone starting, reviewing, or deepening their creative coaching journey.

Andréa Watts is the first specialist in coaching with collage. She founded her practice UnglueYou®, in 2012. With a vision to "See the Collage Coaching Technique™ used globally as a creative coaching tool for releasing people's potential," she shares her knowledge and passion by training coaches and guest lecturing at universities, including City, University of London.

Collage as a Creative Coaching Tool

A Comprehensive Resource for Coaches and Psychologists

Andréa Watts

Routledge
Taylor & Francis Group

LONDON AND NEW YORK

Cover image: Collage by Andréa Watts

First published 2023
by Routledge
4 Park Square, Milton Park, Abingdon, Oxon OX14 4RN

and by Routledge
605 Third Avenue, New York, NY 10158

Routledge is an imprint of the Taylor & Francis Group, an informa business

British Library Cataloguing-in-Publication Data
A catalogue record for this book is available from the British Library

Library of Congress Cataloging-in-Publication Data
Names: Watts, Andréa, author.
Title: Collage as a creative coaching tool: a comprehensive resource for coaches and psychologists/Andréa Watts.
Description: Abingdon, Oxon ; New York, NY : Routledge, 2023. |
Includes bibliographical references and index. |
Identifiers: LCCN 2022004550 (print) | LCCN 2022004551 (ebook) |
ISBN 9780367861230 (hardback) | ISBN 9780367861247 (paperback) |
ISBN 9781003017028 (ebook)
Subjects: LCSH: Personal coaching. | Counseling. | Collage. | Art therapy.
Classification: LCC BF637.P36 W44 2023 (print) |
LCC BF637.P36 (ebook) | DDC 158.3–dc23/eng/20220315
LC record available at https://lccn.loc.gov/2022004550
LC ebook record available at https://lccn.loc.gov/2022004551

ISBN: 9780367861230 (hbk)
ISBN: 9780367861247 (pbk)
ISBN: 9781003017028 (ebk)

DOI: 10.4324/9781003017028

Typeset in Bembo
by Newgen Publishing UK

Dedicated to my mama, Gloria Mills, for telling me the story of the little engine. It has kept me motivated at times when I have faced enormous challenges, including writing this book. Thank you.

Contents

Putting it into Practice   127

Preface

On the surface and when viewed as independent steps, the process of creating a collage appear simplistic, even childish, and belies the psychological significance of each stage. However, when understood and applied as an integrated and progressive approach, its ability to engender transformation is quite extraordinary. Indeed, the very act of creating a collage is metaphorically and literally the act of remaking oneself.

Andréa Watts

Introducing Collage as a Creative Coaching Tool

1 Introduction to Coaching Creatively with Collage

The genesis of this book took root when coaches started asking me how to use collage as a creative tool within their practice. It soon became apparent there was limited information available to support them, because the books that referenced collage related to art therapy or vision boards. As such, this one emerged from a desire to provide a resource for coaches, as well as introduce coaching with collage to the personal development sector where it can be of considerable value to clients.

As an arts-based methodology (ABM), collage is not a new concept for use beyond aesthetic purposes. There are numerous studies and literature relating to its value in therapy, health and well-being, and qualitative research for marketing and academia. All refer to the power of images to access unconscious thinking and allow shifts in mental models through new insights and perspectives. For marketing and research, the emphasis is on its use as a way of eliciting open, honest, and meaningful dialogue, these same outcomes are applicable and beneficial to coaching clients. However, collage is not formally recognised as a standard coaching tool yet, so at the time of writing remains generally overlooked in this field. As the first book dedicated to coaching with collage, the intention is to demonstrate how it fulfils the role of a powerful, creative, and transformative tool to empower clients as they make choices and look to change.

The knowledge I share is accumulated from specialising in coaching with collage since 2012 and developing the tool into the three-stage process named the Collage Coaching Technique™ (CCT). While based on the principles of art therapy and the work of the psychoanalyst Carl Jung, the technique draws heavily on other disciplines and influences that interconnect through the process. They include, amongst others, psychology, creativity, storytelling, metaphors, mindfulness, Clean Language, embodied cognition, and priming. The CCT evolved gradually through my coaching practice, underpinned by research which provided answers to the following questions, "Why do images readily access unconscious thinking?", "What aspects of the process allow clarity and insight for clients?" and "How does it inspire and motivate them to change?". The answers were intriguing, and these explanations and more, combine with my expertise, case studies, and best practice to create an invaluable resource on coaching with collage.

Enriching the Client Experience

Applicable and relevant in every area of coaching, the CCT will deepen coaching conversations and complement your practice regardless of your chosen niche. Furthermore,

DOI: 10.4324/9781003017028-2

practitioners from other disciplines will also find the technique advantageous when working with their client group. In choosing to work with collage, you can expect to enrich your client's coaching experience in the following ways:

- By **accessing unconscious thinking** through images, symbols and metaphors that raise self-awareness and enhance clarity of intentions and aspirations. With this focus, clients create personal goals and objectives that they are more likely to achieve.
- **Connecting emotionally with goals** strengthens personal motivation to make the necessary and sometimes difficult decisions required for success.
- Providing **a non-threatening method** of expressing complex or challenging emotions that, for most clients, initially surfaces unobtrusively as an image.
- The process **quickly uncovers emotional drivers** and mental models that either block or motivate positive change.
- A **sense of well-being** is a key outcome of engaging in an experiential ABM, because it fosters a sense of calm and relaxation through engendering flow and mindfulness.
- As **a tangible output**, the completed collage ensures that clients leave the session with a powerful visual aid for daily motivation and inspiration.
- The **experiential technique** is something that can be witnessed and supported by the coach. As a form of self-directed learning, it empowers and encourages the client to immediately move forward with their new insights.

How to Use This Book

The book is divided into three sections of five chapters each. Grouped according to content, the first provides context. The second focuses on understanding and applying collage as a creative coaching technique, and the last comprises practical guidance and resources, including taking the process online. Each chapter builds on the knowledge and learning from the preceding one to take you on a progressive journey that expands and deepens your comprehension, inspires creativity, and engenders confidence in coaching with collage. While you are encouraged to read the chapters consecutively, there are cross-references (entered as endnotes) to other chapters where you will find more in-depth information on a specific topic, meaning you can read in your preferred order.

Where applicable, each chapter includes relevant theories, the neuroscience and historical background to concepts covered by the CCT. Additionally, the extensive practical guidance includes ideas and descriptions of approaches for you to enjoy learning and implementing with clients. Case studies and client reflections also serve to bring the theory to life and help you better understand and integrate the information. Moreover, the teaching, skills, and approaches in some chapters are transferable to other creative or arts-based coaching methodologies.

The book contains a wealth of material about the process of coaching with collage not found elsewhere. Although a comprehensive resource, it cannot, nor is it intended to replace the benefits of attending a specialist training programme on coaching with collage. For this reason and best practice,[1] while it is possible to work with the technique based on the information in the book, the decision was made not to include a step-by-step guide to delivering the CCT.

Facilitating Engagement

When introducing this creative approach to clients, there may be obstacles to overcome if they:

- believe they are not creative because their understanding of creativity relates solely to the creative sector
- hold a strong belief that they are not visual thinkers
- are fearful or reticent to engage with their unconscious
- are sceptical concerning the use of images for self-development
- have a preconceived idea that the approach is childish

In understanding this, the book equips you with the knowledge to offer advice, reassurance, theories, and science-based evidence to share with clients so that they will trust the process. Additionally, you will be able to explain how the different stages and disciplines combine to access unconscious thinking, raise self-awareness, facilitate clarity, focus, and decision making.

Besides client reservations, you may also feel you have to be an expert in art-making, but this is not the case. The level of your perceived artistic or creative skills is irrelevant. I have met coaches who consider themselves creative and many more who do not. Whichever group you identify with, this book will advance your understanding and confidence so that you can enjoy coaching creatively. At the same time, it will increase possibilities for you to discover and develop your own creativity.

The Terminology Used in This Book

Arts-Based Methods

Used to describe any technique that encompasses elements from 'the arts'. For example, visual arts, poetry, dance, music, and so forth.

Coach

Refers to all practitioners interested in using the CCT as a learning and development tool. Including psychologists, therapists, facilitators, consultants, and counsellors.

Client(s)

Different professions may use alternative words to describe the individual or groups they work with; the word client is used to represent all of these terms.

Collage

In this context, it is a magazine[2] picture collage, rather than a mixed-media version that includes other materials, such as, for example, fabrics. Instead, the collage is created entirely with whole, or fragments of images, words or patterns found in magazines, then glued onto the card.

Visual narrative, composition, and coaching collage are also used as alternative descriptors within the book.

Images

In reference to the CCT, it relates to pictures in magazines or digital images, and includes words, patterns, colours, and shapes. The word 'visuals' is also used as a substitute.

Notes

1 As an immersive, experiential coaching tool that works with the unconscious, rather than applying it from a purely theoretical basis, it is essential to experience it before using it with clients.
2 An online version of the technique is available as a digital alternative. In this case, magazines are replaced by a curated online image library. See Chapter 14 | Coaching with Collage Online.

2   The Author's Story

My story with collage started in childhood, where my passion for art found expression predominantly through this medium.[1] Despite studying art up to higher education and early attempts to forge a career in the creative arts sector, after a few years in retail, I chose to work in the voluntary sector. Nevertheless, having never lost the desire to integrate my passion for art and creativity with assisting others, in 2006, I started an MA Art Therapy course. Here, I learnt about images as a powerful transformational tool and form of visual self-expression by accessing the unconscious mind. Importantly, I also reconnected more deeply to my art practice as we learnt to let go of the aesthetics and focus on the process. Although I did not realise it at the time, this course would significantly influence my career's future direction. At the end of the foundation year, I decided not to pursue the MA, recognising that art therapy was not my path. Consequently, I remained in the voluntary sector.

Time for Change

Although I was valued and had a meaningful role, I felt I should be doing something else, particularly as I became increasingly aware of the lack of opportunities to express my creativity in a visual art form. Furthermore, I missed engaging directly with clients who used the service. External constraints such as funding cuts added more pressure to my role in senior leadership. Consequently, with an awareness that my well-being was declining, I was losing my sense of self, and knowing things could not continue as they were, in early 2012 I saw a careers coach. One of the exercises I completed was a visualisation technique, throughout which I repeatedly talked about doors opening. Because of my artistic background, the coach suggested representing this as a drawing. However, when I tried to, it did not convey what I was trying to express, so I decided to create a collage instead. Having completed the art therapy foundation course, I found myself intuitively working unconsciously. As a result, the visual narrative not only reflected the idea of doors opening; it also contained three key images, all of which were versions of myself, that clearly expressed how I was feeling.

The Girl Under the Blanket

The image of the girl under the blanket resonated so profoundly that I had a physiological response, becoming incredibly upset. It perfectly captured how I had felt hidden, restricted, stuck, and unable to express myself authentically. Previously, I could not find the words to articulate those feelings; now, I knew I had them through the image.

DOI: 10.4324/9781003017028-3

Image 2.1 The Decision | My first personal coaching collage.

The Girl Stretching Her Hand Up

A girl is stretching out her hand as she prepares to remove the blanket. As a version of myself, she confirmed my sense that it was time for me to remove the cover, live the life I was created for and express myself fully. Having decided I was no longer prepared to remain under the metaphorical blanket, this message was inspiring because I knew I was the one who could effect change. When I came across this image, I immediately knew it belonged beside the girl under the blanket, and this is where I positioned her.

The Woman in Red

The woman in red dancing up the stairs reflected the life I desired, being true to myself with the same energy, creativity, flow, freedom, and awareness of the present, precious moments I saw in her. She embraces life and is not afraid to express herself. I intentionally placed her on the stairs, surrounded by white space, with room to move as she dances her way towards the doors.

The Leap of Faith

Together, these three images acted as catalysts that inspired and motivated me to change my career and start UnglueYou®. Determined to make the changes I wanted to see, I took six months to prepare for the transition, assured my new venture would be successful. This belief originated from voluntary experience facilitating a collage session for bereaved carers as part of an annual twelve-week course. Every year, a carer from the preceding cohort was invited to return and share their story to encourage their peers. Each time, in the three years before I started UnglueYou®, these carers returned, unprompted, with their collage. As a visual narrative, each person used it as a tool to share their story, including talking about the changes they had experienced. By the third year, it was clear that the Collage Coaching Technique™ I was developing made a significant impact and would, therefore, likely empower others.

Continual Professional Development

As a lifelong learner, wanting to maximise my potential and provide the best service to clients, I continually develop my skill set. Subsequently, I have undertaken training to complement my arts-based coaching practice, including acceptance and commitment therapy, Clean Language, and mindfulness. Furthermore, with innate curiosity and an appetite for research, I read widely around my area of expertise, encompassing creativity, play, storytelling, art, psychology, visual symbolism, metaphors, and mindfulness.

In academia, I have guest lectured at Kingston University Business School for three years from 2013 on the creativity and leadership module of their MA Management Studies course. A course and module I studied from 2009. Here I used coaching with collage as a visual tool for exploring students' understanding of creativity in leadership. This approach meant that there was an experiential element to their studies alongside the theory that facilitated more in-depth discussion and learning potential. In 2019, I started a position as an honorary lecturer at City, University of London, with their Organisational Psychology department. Additionally, the outcomes of the CCT have been the subject of two research studies by students at the University of Kent and City, University of London.

Respectively, the first focused on *Art and Employment for Maternity Leave and Career Breaks*, while the latter looked at *Mindfulness in Art-Making for Employee Well-being*.

My vision is, "To see the Collage Coaching Technique™ used globally as a creative coaching tool for releasing people's potential." To achieve this vision, I designed and now deliver an International Coaching Federation accredited training programme – *Collage as a Creative Coaching Tool*. Additionally, I speak on the topic with an interactive and highly visual presentation called 'The Science Behind the Art'; as a forerunner to the book, it includes the same subjects of creativity, neuroscience, metaphors, and storytelling.

The Decision and Dance

Named 'The Decision,' I frequently share my first collage story, illustrating how it raised awareness concerning my situation, empowered me to behave differently and make intentional choices about my life's direction. The collage has provided continual learning, including what it means to mature from the girl to the woman, the significant positioning of the three figures in relation to each other and the entire composition, the relevance of the colours blue and red, and my role in being under the blanket. This understanding and the collages I have created since 2012 have undoubtedly enabled me to maximise my potential. My passion for coaching with collage never wanes, fuelled by innumerable clients' stories and the continual personal and professional transformation I experience. Thankfully, the nature of that ongoing change means I genuinely live like the woman in red, and this book results from this life of endless dance.

Note

1 In the context of art, the medium is the material(s) artists use to create their work.

3 Beyond the Vision Board

Understandably, most people are not immediately aware of the distinction between a vision board and the UnglueYou® Collage Coaching Technique™ (CCT). Because both methods use images taken from magazines to create a collage, ostensibly, they appear the same. Additionally, they both generate a tangible output used as an ongoing visual resource to elicit change. However, there remain significant differences concerning the purpose, process, and outcomes.

Vision Boards

Vision boards are so named because the focus is on visualising the future. Their popularity increased after they featured in the book *The Secret*, written by Rhonda Byrne, and Oprah Winfrey endorsed them. Defined by Dictionary.com (2020) as "A collage of pictures, text, and other items that represent and affirm one's dreams and ambitions, created to help visualise and focus on one or more specific aspirations." Therefore, the focus is on identifying goals and ambitions, then creating a visual resource that depicts a future where these aspirations are realised. For this reason, the images, words, ideas, and emotions expressed on vision boards are chosen intentionally to be positive and future-oriented. As a coaching tool, a vision board helps clients focus on what they want for their lives or the year ahead. Sometimes clients are encouraged by the coach to include photos of themselves, draw on their vision board, and add decoration to make it colourful and vibrant. This way, they have something that visually inspires and excites them ("The Coaching Tools Company," 2012).

There are numerous different approaches to creating a vision board, including exercises to help clients connect to and visualise their future before making their board. Usually, coaches are not present while the client creates their board; instead, they may share guidance or a how-to video detailing what to include. While clients are encouraged by some coaches to choose images that resonate with their desired future, predominantly, the instructions are to be intentional in their selection, ensuring they represent their goals. The images can depict material, emotional, physical, and spiritual desires, and some coaches advocate separating these into different areas on the vision board. Many people believe that in creating a vision board they will manifest their future through the law of attraction. Others see them working because, in focusing attention on the images, actions also become focused in that area. Either way, the purpose of creating a vision board is to envision a desired future.

DOI: 10.4324/9781003017028-4

The Collage Coaching Technique™

The CCT is a psychological coaching tool that works from the premise that how people think about themselves and respond to situations affects their capacity to achieve their goals. When clients come to coaching, they may, or may not be aware that they probably face internal conflicts, barriers, and resistance to change. Often rooted in fear, they keep clients stuck in their current situation, unable to move towards their goals and ambitions confidently. Until there is a possibility to identify and face them, these feelings and behaviours impede their ability to create meaningful and sustainable change. However, when self-selecting images, clients may, consciously or unconsciously, avoid things that are challenging. Yet, in that emotional space, where obstacles are revealed and confronted, the opportunity for release and transformation begins. The business name UnglueYou® was chosen to reflect this, with an emphasis on empowering clients to access their unconscious thinking and become 'unstuck.'

Working with the unconscious means, unlike a vision board, clients may come across an image they would not have thought to look for that nonetheless perfectly captures what they need to express. As such, images on their collage include ones they may find challenging or uncomfortable, for example, those relating to past experiences or limiting beliefs and behaviours. Fortunately, they appear on the collage alongside their motivators, strengths, and values, providing clients with a holistic representation of themselves. Furthermore, images clients gather have significant symbolic, metaphorical, and emotional meaning for them. Consequently, besides facilitating the creative process, the coach's role includes working with the client to deepen personal understanding. As a result, new insights and breakthroughs occur for clients as they become aware of their thinking and relationship with themselves and others through their image interpretations. At this stage, increased self-awareness leads to clarity and the capacity and confidence to define their course of action, including desired behavioural change.

To focus and enable relevant material to surface, clients choose a theme[1] for their coaching with collage session. These subjects have included developing resilience, improving well-being, living authentically, career change, returning to work after maternity leave, and building confidence.

Client Reflections | The Difference Between a Vision Board and the CCT

"I've been creating a vision board for my business, once a year, for quite a few years. These are A2 boards on which I stick words and images that represent what I want to achieve in the coming year. I consciously choose the words and pictures from the women's magazines I have at home. Hence these are curated boards which are fun to do and view when I put them on my wall.

I was intrigued when I read about Andréa's collage workshop, and my expectation was that I would create a very similar board. I was wrong! For quite a few reasons – starting with the methodology, then the source of the words and images and lastly the size of the board.

The methodology is very specific and taps into our unconscious emotions and thoughts. The source of the images initially felt more limited, because it excluded the women's magazines I would have consciously chosen. However, this meant I selected more unusual images and words that held my personal interpretation of their meaning. The board is A3 size, which is smaller than my usual vision board, has less on it, yet feels bigger in scope and meaning. It has captured aspects of how I feel about my work and my world in a way I've never captured before (or even thought about). So, I now have a board that I feel inspired by and personally connected to, more deeply than the one I created consciously to fulfil that role. This is the board I have put on my wall, in direct line of sight from my desk – and this board, created using the CCT, is the one that inspires me when I get stuck and reminds me of my purpose and passion. In summary, this smaller board, with fewer images and words, conveys a more intense emotional focus for me." (Lynne Stainthorpe)

Note

1 See Chapter 11 | Facilitating a Safe Space for Coaching with a Creative Technique.

Bibliography

Dictionary.com. (2020). Retrieved May 9, 2020, from www.dictionary.com/browse/vision-board?
The Coaching Tools Company. (2012). Retrieved May 9, 2020, from www.thecoachingtoolscomp any.com/vision-boards-a-great-tool/

4   The History and Application of Collage

Traditionally, collage involves cutting, tearing, and pasting paper or various other materials onto a surface. Predominantly associated with art, the emphasis is on the technique as a method of combining a selection of materials, forms, and sources to create a new visual whole.

Employed by the Chinese after the invention of paper around 200BC, the principle of collage was later used by Japanese artists in the 1100s who stuck paper to silk. However, it was several centuries later before paper collage was first named and recorded in Europe. Originating from the French word *coller,* meaning 'to glue, or to stick together,' it was introduced in 1912 by the Cubist art movement. The term describes when Georges Braque and Pablo Picasso first added found materials[1] and newspaper cuttings to their artwork. This act challenged existing representations in painting, as both artists sought to bring a fresh perspective to the art world (*Georges Braque: Famous Paintings Analysis, Complete Works, & Bio*, n.d.). Since 'perspective'[2] was an established art technique at that time, their artwork mirrored the nature of collage to challenge the norm and offer new ways of seeing, literally and figuratively. Emphasis was on the process rather than the end-product, a position also taken when coaching with collage.

Further evolution in collage techniques occurred as artists began incorporating photographs in their work. These artists were known as Dadaists and coined the term photomontage to differentiate and distance themselves from the Cubist style of collage. They perceived an inextricable link between violence in society and capitalism and focused on portraying and challenging this through their work.

As attitudes and styles shifted in the art world, collage continued to influence artists. In reflecting the unconscious mind, the Surrealist art-movement embraced the medium; exploiting its potential to remake and reframe and take disparate and commonplace objects to create new thought-provoking meaning. Later, these disruptive qualities of collage once more lent themselves as an act of protest. On this occasion, it was the 1970s in Britain, as Peter Kennard made a provocative statement about cruise missiles by adding them to Constable's famous Hay Wain painting (Reilly, 2019).

Where other artistic styles and conventions have gone out of fashion, collage retains its provocative appeal, leading contemporary artists to harness it as a medium for expressing and addressing topical issues. For instance, Yasmine Diaz explores and challenges beliefs around religion and gender, while the late Romare Bearden focused on racial identity. Collage has also made its mark in the digital era, with digital collage artists creating new works using virtual images appropriated from various sources.

From a practical perspective, requiring no artistic skills, collage excels as an easy to access methodology, enabling participation by individuals of any demographic. Online

DOI: 10.4324/9781003017028-5

platforms have also contributed to increasing opportunities for engagement with this versatile medium. No matter how it is used, as a reflection of the artwork it inspires, the collage process constantly unpicks, reshapes, provokes, engages, and renews. Such qualities ensure this medium has an enduring role in capturing and representing individual lived experiences and society generally.

Collage Beyond Art

Though the term collage was first used within artistic circles, the underlying process of combining fragments of knowledge, influences, materials, memories, and so forth to create a new whole transcends visual arts. As such, the principle of collage is expressed in writing, music, architecture, and even life (Fuller, 2016). Writers collate words into sentences and paragraphs, musicians rearrange notes, and life is a collection of myriad experiences.

Aesthetic Application

The collage process enables the development, analysis, reframing, structure, and presentation of information. Therefore, it is ideal when facing issues around surfacing, conceptualising, and verbalising creative ideas. These inherent qualities led to its adoption as a tool by designers, architects and other professions relying heavily on visual information to express ideas and solutions. With digital tools for rendering designs and architectural drawings, the advent of computer technology facilitated collage composition. Believing architectural collage to be more than presenting a visual idea of space, Santibanez (2017, para. 5) said, "The symbolic…associations between fragments of images provide a way to understand all the stories behind a space, transcending the limits of perception to reach an intuitive process." This description comes close to clients' experience of coaching with collage.

On an individual level, collage is also used for creating personal mood boards intended to visually capture ideas around topics such as wedding plans, leisure activities, and interior or garden design. Because mood boards reflect preferences of colour, style, desired ambience, and such like in the finished composition, the images usually retain their original meaning. Where these boards encapsulate dreams and aspirations, they are known as vision boards.[3] While magazines continue to be used to create mood and vision boards, this activity's popularity is reflected in the prevalence of online tools for this purpose. For example, Pinterest, launched in January 2010, provides a platform where users curate and share their thoughts and ideas with images. Closely related to this is the organisation of personal memories, first captured as digital photographs, then arranged using online photo collage software.

Marketing and Brand Identity

Mood boards originated from marketing as a form of qualitative research. Information concerning consumers' honest opinions of a product or service is closely related to unconscious feelings, values, past experiences, and biases. From a psychological perspective, collage facilitates a means to explore and express this complexity. One market research tool designed to access unconscious knowledge through collage is the Zaltman Metaphorical Elicitation Technique (ZMET®). Dr Zaltman developed the technique at the Harvard Business School in the early 1990s (*Olson Zaltman*, n.d.), emphasising the meaning of metaphors in the imagery chosen by market research participants. Through this, the researchers elicit in-depth knowledge of a consumer's relationship with a brand that would be unattainable by words alone. This information determines where brands focus their attention and enables them to influence their customer's behaviour in a meaningful way.

Qualitative Research | Collage as Inquiry

Akin to marketing, within academia, the inherent meaning-making properties of collage caused its appropriation as a research tool. Areas covered are diverse, ranging from studies with refugee and asylum-seeking women, school children envisioning care and support, educational leadership, and the unexplored potential in tourism.

While different methodologies are employed, the qualities of magazine picture collage (and occasionally, more abstract collage) as a visual and projective mode of inquiry underpins every study. From a qualitative researcher's viewpoint, as the intuitive and hidden becomes known, the information that emerges considerably broadens areas for examination (Knowles et al., 2012). An approach further enhanced by facilitating knowledge acquisition through metaphor, narrative, and embodiment.

Notably, the collage process aligns with the perspective and requirement of qualitative researchers to capture the subjective. Collage facilitates this by accessing the unconscious and subduing cognitive thought processes, allowing for greater self-expression and the revelation of knowledge that may otherwise remain unarticulated. Additionally, space is created for the unexplained, contradictory, and unintended to emerge and merge. This type of information provides an exceptional resource for discussion, critical analysis, and clarification by both the participant and the researcher. Consequently, collage is gaining prominence as a mode of research, both on and offline, with Google scholar, to date,[4] returning nearly 56,000 related articles on the subject.

Psychological Development

As a psychological tool, collage has an invaluable role as a therapeutic intervention in art therapy and counselling. Significantly, in this context, the process of collage offers clients a relatively non-threatening means of self-expression and a way to explore profoundly emotional issues (Buchalter, 2004; Malchiodi, 2003). While coaching clients are not expected to present with the same level of emotional need as those in therapy, collage allows the presentation of challenging material in a non-intrusive manner. As described by a client, "I was surprised to find I had uncovered past experiences and deeply held mindsets without even realising it until I began sharing the meaning of my collage." Applicable in individual and group settings, the capacity for exploration in a non-threatening manner also makes collage ideal for use where differing views and perspectives potentially create conflict. Examples include organisational change, new leader assimilation, and supervision.

The Core of Collage

Understandably, with its ability to challenge convention, visualise and present ideas, provide a means to articulate complexity, and enable profound psychological insight, collage has been leveraged for application in diverse fields. Regardless of the context, through disassembling, disrupting, questioning, reassembling, and remaking, the collage process always offers more than what is seen on the surface. Within this broader context, it takes its place as a creative coaching tool.

Notes

1 Found material are commonplace, manufactured, or natural objects (or fragments of such), not intended for art, that are found or scavenged by an artist and may be incorporated into their artwork.
2 Perspective is a technique in art developed in the early 15th Century. It is governed by a set of rules that creates the illusion of depth (3-dimensions) on a flat surface (2-dimensions), such as canvas.
3 See Chapter 3 | Beyond the Vision Board.
4 February 2021.

Bibliography

Buchalter, S. I. (2004). *A Practical Art Therapy* (First). Jessica Kingsley.

Fuller, J. (2016). *Collage and the Creative Process.* https://jarrettfuller.com/projects/collage

Georges Braque: Famous Paintings Analysis, Complete Works, & Bio. (n.d.). Retrieved August 17, 2020, from www.georgesbraque.org/

Knowles, J., Cole, A., & Butler-Kisber, L. (2012). Collage as Inquiry. In *Handbook of the Arts in Qualitative Research: Perspectives, Methodologies, Examples, and Issues* (pp. 265–277). SAGE Publications, Inc. https://doi.org/10.4135/9781452226545.n22

Malchiodi, C. (Ed.). (2003). *Handbook of Art Therapy* (Vol. 31, Issue 3). Guildford Press. https://doi.org/10.1016/j.aip.2004.03.002

Olson Zaltman. (n.d.). Retrieved February 2, 2021, from www.olsonzaltman.com/

Reilly, S. (2019). *Stick 'em up! A surprising history of collage | 1843.* The Economist. www.1843magazine.com/culture/look-closer/stick-em-up-a-surprising-history-of-collage

Santibanez, D. (2017). *12 Offices that Use Collage to Create Architectural Atmospheres | ArchDaily.* www.archdaily.com/784648/12-ways-of-representing-multi-layered-architectural-atmospheres

5   The Collage Coaching Technique™

When clients enlist the support of a coach, they are often seeking direction in their lives because they are uncertain of themselves or their futures. Something is wrong, and they sense it. Frequently this involves emotional pain or fear (even though this may not present itself as the issue) that manifests as blocks and limiting beliefs reflected in their language. They desire to see change but lack the clarity and potentially the confidence to achieve this and are hoping a coach can help them. Fortunately, the answers lie within themselves, meaning the solutions and direction they seek are always available. Unfortunately, daily life and routines often prevent clients from creating the time or space to access these internal solutions, or circumstances have led them to stop trusting themselves. As a result, they lose access to their knowledge and the courage to affect the change they want to see. By providing tools that facilitate their knowing, the coach can help clients reconnect with themselves in a meaningful way and support them in their decisions to transform their lives.

Access Unconscious Thinking

The purpose of the Collage Coaching Technique™ (CCT) is to enable this connection by working with clients using images within a self-directed, projective technique. This approach's value lies in the capacity of images to create a bridge between the unconscious and conscious parts of the mind. As a result, the hidden becomes revealed through bypassing the boundaries that separate internal experiences of external events. Essentially, unconscious thinking is accessed, enabling clients to uncover the mental models and experiences that influence how they feel, think, and behave. This knowledge forms the building blocks of self-awareness that empower focused behavioural change and precede the release of individual potential. Therefore, the focus of exploring internal thought processes is to enable discovery that allows clients to succeed with their intentions and move forward more effectively.

Additionally, through this exploration, clients repeatedly report reaching acceptance of themselves in their current state and situation.[1] This form of acceptance is neither resignation nor capitulation but a laying down of guilt, judgement, and the perception of failure. It is a realisation that they do not have to force change and can want one thing while experiencing another without this being a source of conflict or paralysis. In this emotional space, clients gain a sense of freedom, hope, trust, and confidence in their ability to affect personal change.

DOI: 10.4324/9781003017028-6

Client Reflections | On Acceptance

"After creating my collage, I realised it had definitely helped me with acceptance, with the duality of feeling I had to be having fun, and am I having fun in the right way? Or have I said the right thing in this instance? So, there was this monologue going on in my brain while I was just trying to do stuff or just be in the moment. Looking at the collage reminded me it's okay to be both. So even though the monologue was still happening, I'm not then having one on top of that, thinking – Oh gosh! Why am I behaving like this? Instead, it was just like, be with it as it is, which in turn kind of helped the other voice at least quiet down. I naturally started to relax a bit more with this whole voice thing, and therefore I'd recognise that in situations I would just be more present. I think there's something about acceptance, it definitely creates freedom. You don't realise how much energy you're pouring into battling your emotions that doesn't leave any kind of capacity to grow." (Trinity) (see Figure 9.2.1).

The Collage Coaching Technique™ | The Process

The CCT is a three-stage process within a structured framework. The approach emphasises images, symbols, and metaphors as the key to accessing unconscious thinking. The resources, design, and content of each stage move the client through the creative process. Firstly, taking them on a journey into the unconscious and intuitive knowing, then creating meaning through cognitive evaluation, which facilitates full conscious awareness and integration of learning. As illustrated in Figure 5.1, each stage flows from and builds on the previous one, accompanied by palpable shifts in clients' physiological states. This shift occurs as they move from silent intuition to visual creativity and reflection before the highest energy state of storytelling and the coaching conversation.

The technique is neither art therapy, which addresses psychological disturbances through artistic projections and embodied expression, nor is it psychotherapy that looks back to understand behaviours and reconcile the past to heal and move forward. However,

Table 5.1 The Collage Coaching Technique™ flow chart (Design based on a graphic by Lana Baqaeen)

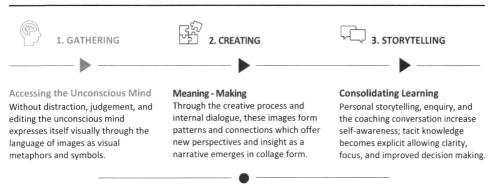

1. GATHERING	2. CREATING	3. STORYTELLING
Accessing the Unconscious Mind	**Meaning - Making**	**Consolidating Learning**
Without distraction, judgement, and editing the unconscious mind expresses itself visually through the language of images as visual metaphors and symbols.	Through the creative process and internal dialogue, these images form patterns and connections which offer new perspectives and insight as a narrative emerges in collage form.	Personal storytelling, enquiry, and the coaching conversation increase self-awareness; tacit knowledge becomes explicit allowing clarity, focus, and improved decision making.

After completing the three-stage process, client discovery, learning, and self-development continue beyond the life of the coaching session. As a tangible visual output, the collage is a resource for ongoing reflection, inspiration, and motivation.

with roots in these disciplines, the CCT adds value to coaching by drawing on aspects from both therapies. Alongside referencing psychology and other techniques, this single tool allows clients to explore the diverse factors that influence their situation, choices, and behaviour. Significantly, through the process, the collage reveals which aspects of themselves and their lives require addressing to resolve the client's issue.

Coaching with Arts-Based Methods

The CCT is an arts-based method (ABM); therefore, the following qualities inherent in such approaches support clients in increasing self-awareness and creating meaningful shifts:

- Artistic expression always involves two forms of self-expression. One is a deliberate and conscious external creative endeavour. The other occurs because the process of creating something always unconsciously reveals aspects of the 'self,' no matter how seemingly insignificant. This characteristic is fundamental to all ABM's, and therefore can be utilised to support clients in accessing a way of knowing that is internal and intuitive.
- When they involve making a tangible object, ABM's elicit knowledge and sources of information through projection, embodied cognition, visual, kinaesthetic, and potentially auditory learning.
- Artistic visual communication equips individuals with the materials and methods that facilitate and empower them to construct their thoughts and emotions.
- Engagement with an art process necessitates a quality of attention that engenders flow and mindfulness. In these states, the client can stay with their exploration longer than they would otherwise, increasing the depth of their reflection and self-directed discovery (Falato, 2012).
- The introduction of an arts approach, particularly for those not used to regular creative artistic expression, causes the brain to work in unfamiliar and diverse ways. According to Gray (2019), this can create new pathways, ways of thinking, feelings, and behaviours.

Furthermore, as an ABM that requires only limited, relatively low-cost resources, the CCT is easily accessible across all demographics and cultures.

Creating Connections

By combining other disciplines, collage is both a rare and unique solution that genuinely facilitates access to numerous learning methods. Consequently, it allows connections on multiple levels and simultaneous processing of different forms of knowledge. These enable clients to experience a truly integrative approach to self-development as images, creativity, mindfulness, embodiment, storytelling and more, form bridges between:

- unconscious and conscious knowledge
- emotive and analytical perspectives
- intuitive and cognitive processes
- internal and external experiences

- practical and spiritual awareness
- tacit and explicit information

Importantly the nature of the process also engenders meaningful personal connections:

- the client and coach partnership of trust develops faster
- group work and sharing the collage beyond the coaching session builds and deepens relationships with colleagues and others

Ultimately, experiencing the process creates the most important connection of all, that of the client to a deeper understanding and acceptance of themselves.

Remaining Open to Possibilities

Neuroscience, theoretical models, and psychology provide thought-provoking and useful explanations for how and why the CCT is an empowering and powerful creative coaching tool. Nonetheless, the nature of working with the unconscious, intuition, and creativity means experiencing the process yields outcomes that are not always readily explained. Therefore, coaching with collage is a space that holds the potential to surprise and delight both client and coach. There is an invitation to remain open to these possibilities without the need for analysis, explanation, or critique. In doing so, opportunities exist to experience a deep awareness available to the human mind, body, and spirit.

Note

1 See case study Figure 7.1.

Bibliography

Falato, D. (2012). *How Using Art Making as a Coaching Tool Supports Client Learning.* International Coach Academy. https://coachcampus.com/coach-portfolios/research-papers/dawn-falato-how-using-art-making-as-a-coaching-tool-supports-client-learning/

Gray, R. P. (2019). *Art Therapy and Psychology.* Routledge.

Coaching with Collage |
The Science Behind the Art

6 The Power of Visual Communication

Visual Communication | A Brief History

For this brief history,[1] the definition of visual communication is given as "The use of images, pictures, symbols, icons, photographs, or videos as the principal format for conveying information, ideas, and emotions."

Throughout humanity's history, visuals have been used as a method to record, preserve, teach, express, and share information. The earliest known form of visual communication dates back over 40,000 years, with cave paintings found in Western Europe and Indonesia. These consist of geometric shapes and simple hand stencils. The first figurative cave paintings are closer to 35,000 years old. Although researchers are yet to determine the exact purpose of these paintings, the assumption is that they were used, as today, to record, preserve, and share information.

Fast forward another 37,000 years, and hieroglyphic symbols (recognisable pictures of the things they represent) used in Egypt bring a formal structure to visual-based communication. Because it was structured, most modern western alphabets descended from or were influenced by the latter.

However, it was not until Gutenberg invented the printing press in 1440–1445 that written material became widely available to a broader reading public. Previously, books were the exclusive property of the elite few who could afford manuscripts and read Latin. Now, for the first time in history, books could be printed and mass-produced at a fraction of the cost of existing methods. Nevertheless, many people were still illiterate, so images continued to be a way of communicating information. For example, at a time when most people regularly attended church, paintings and stained-glass windows served a dual purpose as a decorative light source and to convey core religious ideas. These included teaching the nature of God through the narrative and symbolism seen in the images in the windows.

Photography and Television

Gutenberg's printing press meant the written word became the dominant form of communication until the invention of photography in 1826. Although not an instant transition, within 50 years, images were once more an indispensable medium for transmitting information and communicating ideas, theories, and emotions. The most influential of these occurred within the advertising industry through the media of television, billboards, and magazines. The marketing sector understood the most effective way to

DOI: 10.4324/9781003017028-8

sell products was using images connected to basic human needs and emotions (Davis, 1992). Therefore, advertisers intentionally incorporated images that would provoke an emotional response. This practice continues today, explaining why a significant proportion of research concerning the power of images to affect behavioural change originates from the marketing sector. Equipped with this knowledge, companies can target their intended consumers. For example, there is a difference between images used in advertising campaigns for commercial purposes and those for fundraising campaigns run by not-for-profit organisations. To influence a purchase, the former aims to convey an 'ideal' and therefore uses images that reflect, or create, the societies idea of this state. The latter intends to stir strong, empathic emotions that encourage donations and therefore chooses visuals to evoke such feelings. Regardless of the sector, the purpose is to influence the consumers' choices.[2]

The other media sector where images took a foothold, both in print and television, was journalism. With the invention of the first 35mm camera in 1925, a new genre, known as photojournalism, emerged and burgeoned. Perhaps one of the most compelling examples from that genre is the photograph taken by Nick Ut during the Vietnam War, showing a terrified young girl running naked down the street as she fled from a napalm bomb. An image that not only communicated a story but shaped one by galvanising the anti-war efforts. The potential for images to both tell, and shape stories, has a significant role in coaching with collage.[3]

The Internet

In 1982 the first emoticon (emotions and icons) was used online by Scott Fahlman to help redress the balance of the written word (Ruan, 2011). Although it looked like this, :-), the idea was not to represent a face. Instead, the intention was to convey a feeling, such as happiness or humour. Over time, emoticons developed into emojis. As modern-day hieroglyphics, they express an emotion, idea, or concept without needing explanation. Their continual rise in popularity across all sectors and online platforms is driven by the human desire to share and express feelings as well as words. Alongside words, emojis, gifs and stickers supplement, and at times replace written language.

The spread of the Internet, and the mass-market availability of the Smartphone, with its built-in camera, increased the accessibility of more individual expression through images. Social media sites, particularly YouTube, Pinterest, and Instagram help fuel this growth by designing platforms for sharing information in a predominantly visual format.

Art

Art, which transcends historical timelines, is primarily considered as a way of enhancing the physical environment. However, it is also a powerful method of self-expression, sharing information, conveying ideas, and influencing behaviour. As far back as 375BC, Plato proposed that painters should be banned from the ideal state because he perceived them as a risk, believing artists in any discipline could present false realities and affect the mood and attitude of others (Lee, 1987, as cited in Domke et al., 2002). Throughout the ages, royalty has also capitalised on art as an influential type of communication by commissioning artwork to portray and convey their authority, wealth, and power.

There are, and have always been, those artists who choose to use their art to make a point, impact society, and sway opinion. Two, out of innumerable examples, are Pablo Picasso, with his anti-war painting 'Guernica' and Frida Kahlo's 'Las dos Fridas,' considered a predecessor to identity politics. More contemporary artists include Yasmin Diaz and Romare Bearden, as referenced in Chapter 4.

From a psychological perspective, de Botton & Armstrong (2013) argue that art has a role in conveying ideas that engender mental resilience and influence behavioural change through shifts in mindsets. Thus, they believe artwork can help individuals cope with the challenges and confusion in different areas of modern life, such as relationships and finances.

Art as a form of visual communication is an in-depth topic. Nonetheless, the examples given demonstrate its role extends beyond a purely decorative function. This understanding is impacting the learning and development sector, which is steadily incorporating arts-based methods (ABM) into client work. These approaches, such as visual facilitation, sketch notes, and picture cards, are employed by coaches and facilitators to share or elucidate information, with an awareness that visuals and visual thinking:

- promote the discovery of solutions
- connect people and enable discussion
- convey ideas quickly and easily
- facilitate understanding of complex information

These are all outcomes that are also consistent with coaching with collage.

Images Facilitate Emotional Connection | The Neuroscience

According to Jung et al. (1964, p. 64), "Images are integrally connected to the individual by the bridge of the emotions," without this type of connection, the image is of little consequence to the viewer. The strength of the emotional resonance increases in proportion to an individual's relationship to the image. This effect is caused by how human brains store experiences as memories through a process known as encoding.

Encoding

Creating a memory begins by paying attention, either consciously or unconsciously, to the stimuli perceived through the senses. At this point, neurons start to fire more frequently, increasing the intensity of the experience and, therefore, the probability of it being encoded as a memory (Mastin, 2010). However, this episode must be converted into a format that allows it to be stored for later recall. The storage process that relates to images and visual sensory information is known as visual encoding. It is an ongoing neurological process with evidence to suggest that perception and storage of new visual stimuli and knowledge are significantly influenced by existing mental models, values, and experiences (Domke et al., 2002). Essentially, connecting with and storing images is strengthened where similar encoding already exists. In coaching, this has relevance concerning the potential impact of priming[2] on clients and how learning is consolidated through what is already known, creating linked bundles of data.[4]

Memory Consolidation

The amygdala (located within the medial temporal lobe) and the hippocampus are responsible for memory consolidation, which stabilises new memory before moving it to long-term storage; their roles are as follows:

- the hippocampus – combines sensory perceptions and decides if it is worth committing the experience to memory
- the amygdala – moderates the emotional strength of memory consolidation

As an individual or group experiences an event, the hippocampus determines whether to store it. During this activity, the amygdala's role is twofold, firstly, to decide which emotions to save, secondly, at what intensity level alongside the visual. Research demonstrates how emotional events enhance the function of the medial temporal lobe's memory system. Consequently, these types of events, along with their associated images, are remembered better than neutral ones (Dolcos et al., 2004). Furthermore, the strength of the emotional or physiological reaction at recall reflects the initial encoding intensity.

Visual Resonance

The process of visual encoding explains why images that resonate with clients can evoke a range of intense responses. Essentially, as emotions and visual stimuli are encoded into memory together, seeing the same or similar stimuli recalls the associated experience and feelings, for example, holiday or wedding photographs. This type of remembering is known as episodic, because it refers to personal feelings; as opposed to semantic knowing, which relates to language and concerns impersonal, fact-based recollection. Evidence also suggests emotional resonance does not have to be a result of direct experience. Because the same area of the brain is involved with vision and visual imagination, visual stimuli through the media, or images created internally from a story recounted by someone else, undergo the same encoding process with subsequent emotional effects (Branthwaite, 2002; Gray, 2019). This 'secondhand' effect is enhanced when there is an actual or felt association with the characters, story, or images.

Case Study | The Emotive Power of Images

Helen had recently come out of a long-term relationship. While she had known it was neither healthy nor balanced and had wanted to end it, she had not. Instead, her partner had ended the relationship, leaving her with a sense of rejection. Helen saw this event as the primary reason she had not moved forward with her goals.

During her session, the image of a woman by a pond resonated with Helen. She recalled how it brought back memories of when her mother had fallen in their pond. Although she had not witnessed the event, the image still caused a strong fearful emotional and physiological response. When asked where she felt it, she replied, "In my chest," placing her hands there. (Such visceral reactions provide alternative opportunities for client exploration using, for example, visualisation or other coaching techniques). At the time of the accident, her dad phoned her and to say what happened. As she listened, Helen visualised her mum falling in the pond, and her initial reaction had been one of fear concerning her mum's safety, who fortunately had been unharmed. The image, with its associative memories, triggered the same emotions felt when the accident first occurred. As she recounted the memory to me, she was moved to tears and expressed surprise at the intensity of her emotional and physical response. She was shocked to realise that the memory was still very raw, despite it happening 20 years ago, especially as they had joked about the accident as a family for years.

Sometime after the pond incident, both her parents died within a few months of each other. However, at the time, pregnancy and caring responsibilities meant she felt she had not grieved for them properly. As she continued to use the image to elaborate on this experience, Helen became aware of an ingrained inability to end relationships well; and now believed this stemmed from inadequately grieving for her parents. While speaking and responding to questions, she continued to reflect and process the insight until concluding that it caused her to struggle with endings. This behavioural trait exhibited in relationships and other areas of her life, a connection she had not previously made. Helen decided that this unresolved experience, not her relationship with her ex-partner, had held her back from moving forward positively with her goals. She was surprised but relieved to have reached this conclusion, as with this clarity she could take relevant action, which she decided meant seeing a bereavement counsellor.

Physiological Effects of Visuals

Numerous studies substantiate that the right (referring to eliciting emotional resonance) visual has the power to affect individuals on a physiological level (Branthwaite, 2002; Bresler, 2011; Malchiodi, 2003). Because images work with the unconscious where there is no concept of time, the brain responds to visual triggers as though the related experience were happening in the present moment (Gray, 2019). As illustrated by Helen's case study, this emotional response includes the original physical reactions. All major bodily functions are subject to this involuntary, autonomic response, including changes to heart rate, pupil dilation, blood pressure, and cortisol levels. This type of reaction may be evoked by an actual image or indirectly through visualisation.

When coaching with the Collage Coaching Technique™ (CCT), clients can have a physiological reaction at any stage during the process. Although they are made aware of the possibility of this occurrence, clients remain surprised at the strength of their physical response. These embodied experiences materialise in numerous ways, including smiling, laughter, tears, and intakes of breath. Clients may describe getting goosebumps at a moment of profound insight or a sense of fear and paralysis that manifests as a knot in the chest or elsewhere. Regardless of how they find expression, the physical nature of these responses is now available to explore with clients and often indicate that something important has surfaced.

Image Retention | Assisting Client Development

As explained, emotional experiences improve retention of information, visual stimuli, and memory recall. This neural process contributes to coaching with collage in the following ways:

1   Because clients are using images, there is a faster recollection of their experiences, thoughts, and associated emotions. Once brought to conscious awareness, they are a source of reflection and for facilitating dialogue.

2   As a creative coaching technique, collage results in new perspectives that create, heighten, shift, or change clients' emotional connection with their images. As deeply personal imagery with strong emotional associations, they are likely to be visually encoded together at a high intensity during the coaching process. The nature of this storage level explains clients' long-term retention and recall of their insights and outcomes from the session, an effect that outlasts working with and processing words alone (Burmark, 2002). Moreover, even when the collage is unavailable, this recall and longevity remain the case.

3   Thoughts that might otherwise drift away now anchor to images that act as triggers, reminding clients of their outcomes, insights, breakthroughs, and intentions each time they see their collage. For this reason, having a tangible visual output is a significant benefit of coaching with collage.[2]

Client Reflections

"After completing my collage, I put it up in my kitchen next to the fridge and reflect on it daily. One of the most powerful images is of a lady with a drawn bow and arrow which serves as constant reminder to me to stay focused on my goals. The centre piece is a close-up picture of a moth, which is a reminder to confront my fears! I also have motivational quotes such as, 'Take control and live the life you want,' alongside beautiful images of nature and celebrations which I find energising and uplifting.

The three collages that I have created since 2016, contain symbols and themes from which ideas can continually be developed and it really has helped me to maintain a visual image of my values.

By regularly reflecting on these images, I believe it serves to help me overcome my challenging emotions, remain optimistic and positive about the future. Also, using my imagination and creativity to evoke interests which are not immediately obvious, but have emerged over time and understanding aspirations that I would like to come to fruition. Such as more leadership, visibility and self-expression in my career, organising a family trip to Guyana and finding love and true companionship." (Michelle)

Defamiliarising the Familiar

Despite language helping to shape interactions, it also has limitations (Bento & Nilsson, 2009). Therefore, as the default communication mode, it reduces the chances of new insights and perspectives emerging for clients as they continue to process their thoughts, concerns, and emotions from a primarily evaluative and rational perspective. In doing so, they exclude what is available at the unconscious and intuitive level. In contrast, through expression at a preconscious level, visuals allow direct access to material and emotions that override cognitive censorship (Branthwaite, 2002). Furthermore, they fulfil the function of 'defamiliarisation,' a phrase coined by Shklovsky (1917). This individual was a Russian artist who argued that representing and then reflecting on the familiar in an unfamiliar way, breaks the thinking patterns and behaviour that overlook and reduce experiences to a series of unconscious habits. For example, using imagery to facilitate dialogue, and collage as a form of expression rarely, if ever engaged with by clients, compels alternative perspectives, requires lengthier engagement with the topic, and offers new insights.

Facilitating Open Dialogue

Verbal communication requires conscious thought to order information and share it in a way that can be understood by the listener (Branthwaite, 2002). Because verbal interactions primarily occur at this cognitive level, there is always a possibility that the speaker will filter out information, either consciously or unconsciously, that they do not want the listener to know. Reasons for this may be fears around being judged or appearing foolish. Equally, they may struggle to articulate abstract concepts, challenging thoughts, or painful emotions. From a coaching perspective, this means that using verbal communication alone may require several sessions before the client feels comfortable sharing openly. However, using images reduces cognitive editing, in turn facilitating more immediate and candid dialogue.

Case Study

During her first coaching session, Karen shared an image from her collage that held strong resonance. It represented her desperate desire as a child for her mum's attention that she described as distracted elsewhere, essentially by her partner. By the time it came, Karen said it was too late, as she was already emotionally damaged.

The image reflected a duality of emotions as she interpreted it as a mother and child, seeing herself in both. From age nine, she unwillingly took on the mother role for her younger brother and acutely felt her lost childhood with the resulting challenges. As such, the mother figure's stance spoke to her of intentionally turning away with disinterest, echoing her mother's attitude towards her and Karen's in not wanting to take on parenting responsibilities. The child held the yearning she felt looking towards her mother, desiring acknowledgement and attention, mirrored by her younger brother's behaviour towards her. Karen concluded by describing her childhood as leaving her feeling tired, angry,

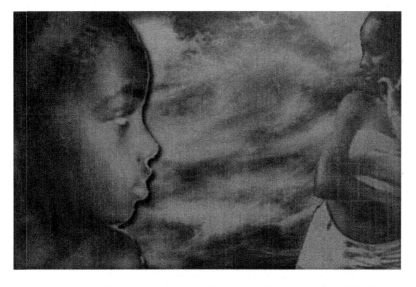

Figure 6.1 Cropped section representative of Karen's collage, seeing herself in both figures.

alone, afraid, and lacking confidence, adding how the absence of colour in the image evoked these emotions perfectly.

Facilitated by imagery, Karen had shared a profoundly personal experience that was detrimentally impacting her decision making. Before the session ended, she decided to forgive her mother in an attempt to reconcile her past and build self-confidence. In identifying the change needed to overcome her challenging issue and immediately choosing to try and resolve it, Karen was able to explore her intended goals sooner and improve her pace of progress.

Karen's is an example of when an insight gleaned early on in the coaching process accelerates clients' breakthroughs. Essentially by empowering them to redirect and channel their energy on achieving their goals, rather than focusing on unhelpful thoughts and behaviours or past wounds.

Visual and Verbal Comparative Processing | Facts and Figures

The core differences between how the human brain processes images, compared to words, are summarised below in Table 6.1. These distinctions seem contradictory; nonetheless, they complement and balance each other. Using both visual and verbal communication, the CCT is an integrated approach enabling clients to benefit from the outcomes of the different processing methods. From accessing their intuitive unconscious and analytical conscious knowledge to the other functions detailed in Table 6.1.

Online, the most quoted visual statistic attributed to 3M Corporation[5] is that "We process visual information up to 60,000 times faster than text." Although this particular figure is unsubstantiated, there remains sufficient academic research to evidence the power and efficacy of visual processing. Key findings include that the human brain has the capacity to:

- remember images 72 hours after looking at them with 90% accuracy and 63% recall a year later (Brady et al., 2008)
- understand the sense of a complex natural visual scene in 3/20 of a second (Thorpe et al., 1996)
- process images simultaneously, while language, written and verbal, is processed in a linear, sequential manner (Branthwaite, 2002; Knowles, Cole, & Weber, 2012)
- process 45 bits per second when reading, so a relatively short sentence. Whereas the visual system can cope with 10 million bits per second (Dijksterhuis, 2004)
- comprehend a visual in 13 milliseconds (Potter et al., 2014)

Table 6.1 Comparative processing

Imagery	Verbal
Holistically	Linear-sequentially
Pre-conscious and conscious	Conscious, attentive processing
Intuitive, associative	Rational, evaluative
Involving, automatic (empathy)	Controlled, analytical
Episodic Knowing	Semantic Knowing

Reprinted with permission from "Investigating the power of imagery in marketing communication: evidence- based techniques," by Branthwaite, A, 2002, Qualitative Market Research: An International Journal, 5, p. 168

When considered collectively, these statistics are testimony to the power of images. For clients, the incredible processing capacity of visuals, compared to verbal communication, lends itself to faster perception, enhanced information recall, and improved understanding of complex issues and emotions.

The Overview

This chapter begins by focusing on the history of visual communication before explaining its role and benefit as a form of client self-expression, insight, and personal breakthrough that leads to clarity and action. Significantly, because relating to visuals is a biological process, this approach benefits clients regardless of their preferred learning style, circumstances, demographics, culture, or language. Therefore, every client has the potential to experience immense value from using imagery and collage during their coaching journey.

Notes

1 It should be noted that most of this historical context is based on information related to western culture. Therefore, it does not necessarily reflect the timeline or experience of other parts of the world.
2 See Chapter 7 | Working With the Unconscious (section on primers).
3 See Chapter 9 | Part 2: The Creative Process as an Expression of 'Self'.
4 See Chapter 8 | Part 1: Symbols and Metaphors for Meaning-Making and Self-Awareness.
5 After thorough investigation, I have been unable to source the original research to evidence this statistic. As such, I chose to omit it from the list of substantiated findings and will not quote it in the future.

Bibliography

Bento, R. F., & Nilsson, W. O. (2009). *(PDF) Visual Metaphors: A New Language for Discovery and Dialogue.* Teaching & Learning Journal. www.researchgate.net/publication/254967238_Visual_Metaphors_A_New_Language_for_Discovery_and_Dialogue

Brady, T. F., Konkle, T., Alvarez, G. A., & Oliva, A. (2008). Visual long-term memory has a massive storage capacity for object details. *Proceedings of the National Academy of Sciences of the United States of America, 105*(38), 14325–14329. https://doi.org/10.1073/pnas.0803390105

Branthwaite, A. (2002). Investigating the power of imagery in marketing communication: Evidence-based techniques. *Qualitative Market Research: An International Journal, 5*(3), 164–171. https://doi.org/10.1108/13522750210432977

Bresler, D. E. (2011). *Physiological Consequences of Guided Imagery.* Practical Pain Management. www.practicalpainmanagement.com/treatments/complementary/biobehavioral/physiological-consequences-guided-imagery

Burmark, L. (2002). *Visual Literacy | Learn to See, See to learn.* Association for Supervision and Curriculum Development.

Davis, J. F. (1992). Power of Images: Creating the Myths of Our Time. *Center for Media Literacy.* www.medialit.org/reading-room/power-images-creating-myths-our-time

de Botton, A., & Armstrong, J. (2013). *Art as Therapy.* Phaidon.

Dijksterhuis, A. (2004). Think different: The merits of unconscious thought in preference development and decision making. *Journal of Personality and Social Psychology, 87*(5), 586–598. https://doi.org/10.1037/0022-3514.87.5.586

Dolcos, F., LaBar, K. S., & Cabeza, R. (2004). Interaction between the amygdala and the medial temporal lobe memory system predicts better memory for emotional events. *Neuron, 42*(5), 855–863. https://doi.org/10.1016/S0896-6273(04)00289-2

Domke, D., Perlmutter, D., & Spratt, M. (2002). *The primes of our times? An examination of the "power" of visual images. Journalism,* 3(2), 131–159. https://doi.org/10.1177/146488490200300211

Gray, R. P. (2019). *Art Therapy and Psychology.* Routledge.

Jung, C. G., Henderson, J. L., Jacobi, J., Jaffé, A., & Franz, M.-L. vo. (1964). *Man and his Symbols* (C. G. Jung & M.-L. vo. Franz (eds.)). Aldus Books Ltd.

Knowles, J., Cole, A., & Weber, S. (2012). Visual Images in Research. In *Handbook of the Arts in Qualitative Research: Perspectives, Methodologies, Examples, and Issues* (pp. 42–54). SAGE Publications, Inc. https://doi.org/10.4135/9781452226545.n4

Malchiodi, C. (Ed.). (2003). *Handbook of Art Therapy.* Guildford Press. https://doi.org/10.1016/j.aip.2004.03.002

Mastin, L. (2010). *Memory Encoding.* The Human Memory. https://human-memory.net/memory-encoding/

Potter, M. C., Wyble, B., Hagmann, C. E., & McCourt, E. S. (2014). Detecting meaning in RSVP at 13 ms per picture. *Attention, Perception, and Psychophysics,* 76(2), 270–279. https://doi.org/10.3758/s13414-013-0605-z

Ruan, L. (2011). Meaningful Signs-Emoticons. *Theory and Practice in Language Studies,* 1(1), 91–94. https://doi.org/10.4304/tpls.1.1.91-94

Shklovsky, V. (1917). 'Art as Technique.' In *Art as Technique* (pp. 1–7). https://warwick.ac.uk/fac/arts/english/currentstudents/undergraduate/modules/fulllist/first/en122/lecturelist-2015-16-2/shklovsky.pdf

Thorpe, S., Fize, D., & Marlot, C. (1996). Speed of processing in the human visual system. *Nature,* 381(6582), 520–522. https://doi.org/10.1038/381520a0

7   Coaching with the Unconscious

The term 'unconscious thoughts' refers to those processes, memories, and feelings that occur without conscious awareness. In contrast, 'conscious thoughts' are intentional, controllable, and individuals are aware of them while undertaking a task (Bargh & Morsella, 2008; Dijksterhuis, 2004).

Although the human brain's capacity to hold and process multiple events in conscious awareness is limited, the sum of these experiences is not lost. Instead, cognition, feelings, experiences, memories, and thoughts encountered on a conscious level are stored in the unconscious part of the mind. According to Jung et al. (1964), here they continue to exist as temporarily obscured thoughts, impressions, and images. However, despite residing beyond conscious awareness, they still exert influence over how a person evaluates and responds to others and external situations. Even though people are generally unaware of this impact, unconscious thoughts are understood to be the driving force behind human behaviour and decision making (Bargh & Morsella, 2008; Gray, 2019; Nisbett, 2017).

Accessing the Unconscious Mind in Coaching

Because the content of the unconscious mind exists below the surface of conscious awareness, the wealth of valuable information it contains is not readily available to clients. Most often explained through the analogy of an iceberg, the tip is described as conscious processing, visible and accessible; while unconscious thoughts constitute the vast unseen that lies beneath. During one of his keynote addresses, Lakoff (2015) stated that the latter is estimated to encompass 98 per cent of thinking, or potentially higher.

Out of sight, these hidden thoughts can impact clients' ability to make effective decisions, affect behavioural change, and move forward with their aspirations. For example, thoughts around imposter syndrome, low self-esteem, feelings of guilt, and loss of identity may originate in the unconscious mind. These beliefs and emotions have a detrimental effect on confidence. Conversely, empowering thoughts related to values, self-efficacy, intrinsic motivation, goals, and aspirations emerge from the same source. However, until any of them exist as conscious awareness, none are available to be understood, utilised, or modified. Fortunately, there are coaching techniques to access unconscious thinking and reveal internal drivers.

Images | The Language of the Mind

The most effective means of accessing the unconscious relies on the use of imagery. Drawing on findings from multiple researchers, Bento & Nilsson (2009, p. 1) summarise

DOI: 10.4324/9781003017028-9

that when working with the unconscious "we need to use the language of the mind; a language which is metaphorical, non-verbal, multi-sensorial and teeming with images." Consequently, being predominantly visual in nature, the language of the unconscious is difficult to access using a verbal centred approach. The analogy of travelling to a country where the language is different and not spoken by the visitor, conveys the relationship between the spoken word and the unconscious mind. Until approached with a language it recognises communication is difficult and stilted. However, use one it readily understands, and it shares a wealth of information that finds expression through its visual language. While this language is often symbolic and metaphorical, it remains the starting point for accessing unconscious thoughts and eliciting meaning. While Jung saw symbols in dreams[1] as the essential process for carrying these visual messages from the unconscious intuitive to the conscious rational part of the mind, coaching with collage utilises magazines as the vehicle to enable personal symbolic and metaphorical images to surface.

Enhancing the Connection with Music

Music is proven to influence the human brain in similar ways to images by lowering defences,[4] facilitating access to the unconscious, enabling insights, increasing creativity, and problem-solving (Bush, 1995, as cited in Beebe & Wyatt, 2009). Helen Bonny used these qualities, combining music and visualisation to develop a therapeutic tool in 1970. Known as "The Bonny Method of Guided Imagery and Music," it allows clients to explore, make meaning and integrate their experience in a non-directive manner. While not designed as a therapeutic tool, the Collage Coaching Technique™(CCT) works similarly and can therefore capitalise on the benefits of integrating music alongside visuals to enhance clients' ability to access their unconscious mind. Furthermore, like images, according to Heshmat (2019), music engages multiple parts of the brain to generate connections and associations.

Decision Making and the Unconscious

Clients often seek coaching around subjects that involve making complex choices, and because the conscious mind can make poor decisions (Dijksterhuis, 2004), working with the unconscious can prove invaluable. Complex decisions, by definition, involve processing and analysing multiple pieces of information. However, conscious thought is not well-adapted for this task, having a low capacity for processing numerous pieces of information at once. Instead, it tends to be highly focused but not very inclusive, relying heavily on knowledge easily articulated with words, and consequently overlooks what is harder to verbalise or access (Dijksterhuis, 2004; Nisbett, 2017). This limited focus comes at the expense of other relevant information sources, such as abstract thoughts and emotions. The latter is notable as research has found the role of emotions, which influence judgement and choices, to be particularly influential when making meaningful life decisions (Lerner et al., 2015). Therefore, as clients consciously weigh up the pros and cons, because information that affects their choice is missing, the decision-making process is flawed. Only in combining conscious awareness of internal drivers such as emotions, alongside mental models and rational cognitive appraisal, can a complete picture emerge concerning their situation.

Accordingly, the often difficult and challenging decisions clients are trying to make are best served by combining knowledge from the unconscious and conscious mind.

This holistic approach ensures consideration of important, potentially life-changing choices, is taken with personal, in-depth, and integrated insight. The CCT supports this type of complex decision-making process, first, by accessing unconscious thinking, then by engaging the conscious, rational mind in meaning-making. By enabling exploration of the analytical and emotional together, the process reconnects knowledge with feelings and recognises the latter as a legitimate source of information, learning, and guidance.

Client Reflections: Returning to Work After Maternity Leave

This client's experience illustrates how coaching with collage enables reflection and consideration of both internal and external influences concerning complex decisions, such as returning to work after maternity leave.

"I've created two collages with Andréa, both were after the birth of my children. The first was a 1-1 consultation, the second took place during a group session. On both occasions I appreciated the opportunity to engage with my thoughts and feelings creatively. Finding the process engaging, insightful, useful, and fun.

My first coaching session was to do with going back to work after 6 months on maternity leave. My collage was really helpful in terms of illustrating the mess that was in my head and that I was feeling emotionally. It was quite a colourful collage and I was at the centre of it. There were all these words about trying to juggle and questions like would I be a good mum? Being able to channel all that anxiety and worry creatively and have

Figure 7.1 First Collage by Astrid.

it there on my collage really helped me to express, identify, understand, and make sense of the mess.

During the discussion about the collage, Andréa and I explored the themes coming out of my collage. Including how I define a good mum and making the logistics work between home and work life. This was particularly important as I felt I had no choice but to go back to work. But then we talked about the silhouette image. The one where an orange hand is holding the wrist of the turquoise figure with both arms raised. Andréa asked me 'If I were one of them, which would I be?', I replied 'both.'

I often have the challenge of two conflicting emotions and desires. Wondering how I reconcile them and go on? In this case it was about wanting to remain at home with my daughter while at the same time needing to return to work. Being able to say this out loud helped me understand that it was OK to return to work. I enjoyed my profession and had worked hard to reach my position of senior lecturer. Becoming aware of and accepting this helped me feel more confident about returning to work.

Also, importantly it was about accepting it was going to be hard and that I wasn't going to be perfect in either role. There'd be days when I'd juggle and days when I'd do one thing better than the other and that was OK.

So, after the birth of my second child when I was experiencing a lot of challenges going back to work, I joined a group workshop. The timing was serendipity because I was having a really, really difficult time. I had a feeling that I had lost my professional identity. I had all these different thoughts in my head

- Shall I go back after having my second child?
- Shall I stay in academia?
- Should I change my career?
- Should I stay in academia and shorten my hours?
- Should I change my career and shorten my hours?

These multitude of decisions I could make were overwhelming me.

Maybe that's why the collage I created was very different to the first one. Visually it was a lot darker in that one side was just black. However, it also included a flap I could open and under that was positivity. So, although I'm not there yet, I thought there's light at the end of the tunnel.

The discussion was super helpful in allowing me to realise that it was ok to be searching and not have the answers yet. That I can be in the state of flux and ride it out. I know it sounds simple when I say it out loud. But at the time I had a strong sense of 'I need to decide, I need to fix it!' and this was causing me anxiety and stress.

Both collages were important experiences and helped me to ride that wave. They helped me to make sense of my situation in terms of how I was feeling and gave me an opportunity to think about some of those things creatively and come to a resolution. On both occasions the resolutions were around acceptance. This was important because although a part of my anxiety was coming from the things that were stressing me out, a big part was coming from my sense of the need to fix it, find a solution and make things better. It was helpful for me to reach an understanding that it's ok not to have a solution. This meant that whereas before I was anxious wanting to decide, fix and control; now I knew that I didn't have to and that's ok. Part of that realisation was knowing it's ok to be doing something but want something else instead. Rather than being stuck with inertia because of thoughts of which one? which one? which one?" (Astrid)

Problem Solving

Research relating to the unconscious and its inherent problem-solving qualities refers predominantly to the incubation period (Lubart, 2001). During this time, an individual's focus is not on the problem, so at some point, without prompting, the unconscious has an opportunity to provide a solution. The moment this new information becomes available on a conscious level is known as 'illumination,' or more commonly, an 'a-ha' moment. The capacity to problem-solve arises from the unconscious mind's ability to continue thinking about important matters, even in the absence of conscious appraisal, a phenomenon where the phrase 'sleep on it' may originate. This state reflects where the unconscious remains active while conscious thoughts become dormant. Although it is not necessary to be asleep, the understanding is that during the incubation period, as the conscious mind is occupied elsewhere, the unconscious processes multiple associations relating to the problem. After this, it reveals promising ideas and solutions to the conscious mind for evaluation. For this reason, incubation and illumination are also recognised as steps in the creative process.[2]

In allowing access to the unconscious, the first stage of the CCT (when clients gather their images) effectively serves as a 'facilitated incubation' period. This suspension of analytical thinking occurs after clients have first tried to resolve their problems using rational, cognitive thinking. Essentially, before seeking coaching. To enable focus during this stage, a theme[4] is agreed, originating from a discussion with the individual client or group. The chosen subject then acts as a:

- **primer:** referred to later in this chapter
- **container:** minimises the probability that distressing or overwhelming experiences hidden by the unconscious will surface[3,4]
- **creative constraint:** provides limitations that reduce complexity and enhance creative expression[2]

The incubation period fulfils a significant role in clients' learning and development beyond their coaching session. Through ongoing processing and reflection on the images in the collage, over time, the unconscious mind reveals further insights and understanding. These revelations may be triggered at any time, including as clients recount their story, when seeing associative words or images, or via an embodied experience.

Andréa's Personal Reflections | A-ha Moments

"Six months after my business started, I created a collage with the theme 'vision and values.' During the gathering stage, without understanding why, I felt a strong resonance towards an image that featured three men, dressed like Formula One mechanics, holding a Michelin tyre. Although I didn't know what it meant, with a strong urge to include it and sensing it had relevance regarding the theme, I incorporated it within my collage. As always, to ensure I saw it regularly, it was placed on a wall in my office. I also shared the story with family, friends, and colleagues, including referencing the image I didn't understand. Three weeks later, while engaged in writing a blog post, I glanced up at the collage and experienced 'illumination' concerning it as a representation of the business I aspired

Figure 7.2 UnglueYou® Vision and Values.

to build. One that would be a well-known brand with durability, while providing out-standing performance and a high-quality service, just as I perceived Michelin tyres. The incubation period allowed time for my unconscious to process the image before revealing its meaning on a conscious level. This knowledge still informs my decision making around business development, while the image serves as a constant reminder of my aspirations for UnglueYou®." (Andréa–Author)

Providing New Information

The unconscious mind contains material that was not acquired consciously, which means new information can emerge from it. From a Jungian perspective, this phenomenon relates to the collective unconscious, a level of unconsciousness shared by humanity and groups of people[5] that exists independently of the individual (Jung et al., 1964). It contains latent ancestral, and universally recognised memories, instincts, archetypes, and symbolism.

Bargh & Morsella (2008) reference research concerning adaptive learning that aligns with Jung's theory. The suggestion is that predispositions and intuitive responses are (besides via childhood and culture) gradually learnt through evolution and refined as they are carried forward over generations. In existence as prior knowledge, this information aids understanding of those actions that are helpful versus those that pose a risk, as seen through the fight or flight response. Although people are unaware of the source, these behaviours act as guides, negating an individual's need to determine their reactions to cer-tain situations. Similarly, Gray (2019) references epigenetics research, which relates to her-editary behaviours that originate from biological changes in gene expression. Influenced by the environment and experiences of an intense nature, the psychological effects of these alterations are carried forward, affecting future generations. A powerful example of this is the holocaust. Here, there is now evidence that transgenerational effects of trauma on the children and grandchildren of survivors are to some degree due to epigenetics (Kellermann, 2013).

Research in adaptive learning and epigenetics suggests that knowledge and experiences are not known solely through an individual's lifetime. Rather, they are inherited and passed down from one generation to the next. Despite never having experienced the event themselves or explicitly sought information, descendants hold this knowledge without conscious awareness. Therefore, although writing in 1964, J. L. Henderson's description of the collective unconscious as "The psychological inheritance of man" (Jung et al., 1964, p. 107) would appear apt. Furthermore, many non-western cultures share similar philosophies on inheriting ancestral knowledge and the concept of a collective psyche. For these reasons, the unconscious is a valuable resource of accumulated knowledge and information not shaped by personal experience yet available to access.

Priming

"Priming is the presentation of stimuli that makes specific emotions or concepts more accessible to an individual's working memory and can influence both cognition and behaviour without the individual's conscious awareness" (Minas & Dennis, 2019, p. 231). Presented via visual, auditory, and other senses, the different forms of priming include subliminal and supraliminal. While subliminal priming occurs below the threshold of consciousness, the latter is perceived consciously, in advertising for example (albeit without knowing the intended outcome). However, with both forms, the influence and effects take place unconsciously. As the process of coaching with collage starts at an unconscious level, clients' gathered images potentially include ones that, if not a direct result, are at least shaped by priming.

Priming and Behaviour

Every day, clients are exposed to vast amounts of data that may impact their perception of themselves, society, and their role within it. This stimulus, including words, is predominantly presented in a visual format.[6] As a form of communication encountered through multiple channels, this imagery is pervasive. Consequently, even though visual priming tends to have a much stronger impact than other forms of priming, as an intrinsic part of daily life, their capacity to affect and persuade is rarely considered or understood (Elgendi et al., 2018). Like visual communication, a considerable amount of research on this topic originates within the marketing and advertising sector. Therefore, it is unsurprising the content created in these fields intends to psychologically influence or reinforce the viewer's belief systems, decision making, emotions, and so on.

While some studies suggest primers have a more significant influence when reinforcing existing mindsets, values, and assumptions (Domke et al., 2002), others indicate that repeated priming with emphasis on a topic can directly modify preferences or mental models. Despite this difference, both views acknowledge the potential of primers to strengthen or influence individuals' cognitive and emotional behaviour. Furthermore, the suggestion is that, like a domino effect, emphasis on a particular idea can shape how an individual perceives other topics. Therefore, one can reasonably assume that while clients gather images that resonate with them, there is a risk that not all will reflect their actual values and preferred behaviours. Instead, they may represent societal, work, or familial expectations and norms, as illustrated in the following example.

Client Reflections

"I've included the image of a bag with tassels on my collage as I'd love to buy one, but won't because that's not what 60-year-old women do, is it? Everyone thinks I'm strait-laced, but I'm not, not really. I was horrified when my son-in-law laughed when he saw me coming down a slide with my grandson. He said he'd never seen anyone come down a slide being so rigid and conservative before. Then he said he wasn't surprised because that's how I am all the time. It makes me so angry because I feel like I'm behaving in a way that's acceptable to others while not being true to myself. I'd love a bag with tassels, but I don't want people to think I'm mutton dressed as lamb!" (Sandra)

While it is not possible to state conclusively that this client's views resulted from priming, her behaviour was clearly influenced by external ideas concerning being a woman in her early 60s. These views were contrary to how she perceived and wanted to express herself, yet they still affected her decision not to purchase a tasselled bag. Through reflection, storytelling and the coaching conversation, clients can explore, scrutinise, and evaluate the meaning of their emergent images. As these thoughts and perceptions develop into conscious awareness, clients can reflect to differentiate between those that accurately represent their values and preferred behaviours and those that may result from priming or other sources.

The Collage Theme as a Primer

As stated earlier in the chapter, before clients begin work with the CCT, they decide on a theme. As a primer, it functions to stimulate the unconscious (in its 'facilitated incubation' state) to access thoughts, memories, and knowledge related to the subject clients want to explore. This first step increases the probability that whatever is retrieved and made available contains relevant solutions and insights as well as offering breadth, depth, and diversity. Because long-term memory stores related information in bundles, as clients gather images, each one acts as an associative trigger for unlocking connections and networks of understanding and knowledge. Moreover, the metaphorical nature of images allows seemingly disparate bundles of concepts to emerge together.[7] Contrary to how it may appear on the surface, the relationship between these images and what they convey is congruent, as demonstrated by clients' ability to create meaningful narratives.

The Collage as a Personal Primer

Because the completed collage represents clients' mental models, emotions, insights, and decisions, it serves as a personal visual primer. Research in priming on the ability of positive and negative words to influence mood, which in turn affect behaviour, concludes that repeated exposure to either type of word engenders the related emotional state (Minas & Dennis, 2019). Therefore, with clients' collages including affirmative words and images, these findings support its effectiveness as a resource for motivation and inspiration, explaining why clients report an increase in their positive outlook and actions. Even though their collage often includes images they experience as uncomfortable or challenging, these still positively influence clients' behaviour by acting as push motivators, reminding them what they want to change. Due to the effects of repetitive priming, clients are encouraged to place their collage where they will see it regularly.

Client Reflections

"Just looking at it brought me joy. Having it there, not even necessarily absorbing it every day, but like in the book 'Feel the fear and Do it Anyway,' I'm sure it's like subconscious assimilation. I think having it on my wall really helped me take a step forward, even to begin looking for a new job, if I'm honest. Then, once I started a new job being able to navigate quite how difficult that was for me, because when I created my collage, it was with an understanding that it would be scary, whatever it might be. I knew I would do things that would be challenging and new to me, but that would be okay. So, I think the collage reminded and helped me reconcile that so that it wasn't overwhelming. It was still hard changing jobs, but it wasn't overwhelming." (Trinity) (See Figure 9.2.1).

Primers can be more effective influencers when reinforcing existing intentions, making them beneficial when goal-setting (Karreman et al., 2006 as cited by Elgendi et al., 2018). Ergo, as a personal primer, clients are inclined to fulfil their goals because the collage content aligns with their current aspirations. Because it is visual, there is a strong emotional connection that causes the collage to maintain the client's interest and focus (Domke et al., 2002), increasing their likelihood of remaining committed to their intentions. The following short story from a group workshop is one of the numerous examples of priming contributing to clients' impetus to pursue their goals. In this example, the client's decision to act, based on their collage, was immediate.

Client Reflections

"Thank you for the session you ran at the course I'm attending. I was surprised how much I enjoyed the activity and how insightful it turned out to be! I put the collage on my bedroom wall and when I woke this morning it somehow pushed me to make inquiries on reaching my goals. After some phone calls I have an interview for an access to higher education course so I can take a step towards my degree."

I asked the participant to keep me informed of his progress and the next week I received the following email, "I passed the interview and have been offered a place on the course. I honestly believe the collage and our conversation on the meaning stoked a fire in me!" (Marcus)

Overall, the capacity of priming to influence behaviour on an unconscious level has three significant areas of impact in the CCT:

1 Subliminal and supraliminal priming clients encounter every day may affect the images they gather.
2 The theme as primer aids in the focused retrieval of unconscious knowledge.
3 As a personal visual primer, the collage acts as a resource to motivate and help clients fulfil their goals.

Below the Tip of the Iceberg

Based on the premise that the unconscious is the driving force of human behaviour, accessing this breadth and depth of knowledge is vital for clients to achieve meaningful and sustainable change. By focusing on unlocking and retrieving this material through images, the unconscious reveals internal drivers, mental models, and emotions that positively influence or impede personal development. As a visual approach, the CCT is a quick yet powerful coaching resource to enable this outcome. Moreover, once accessed, working with the unconscious introduces a holistic approach to problem-solving and complex decision-making, issues clients typically present. Additionally, the collective unconscious offers opportunities for broader exploration and priming facilitates the ongoing benefits of coaching with collage. When understood in these terms, there is a clear and compelling case for accessing the unconscious mind as an invaluable resource that empowers clients on their coaching journey.

Notes

1　In later years Jung used mandalas to explore the unconscious.
2　See Chapter 9 | Part 1: A Compelling Case for Creativity in Coaching.
3　If the CCT is used in a therapeutic setting, a theme may be agreed with the client that allows traumatic or emotionally painful experiences and thoughts to surface. However, this is not the intention in coaching.
4　See Chapter 11 | Facilitating a Safe Space for Coaching with a Creative Technique.
5　These groups may be based on culture, ethnicity, and faith for example.
6　See Chapter 6 | The Power of Visual Communication.
7　See Chapter 8 | Part 1: Symbolic and Metaphors for Meaning-Making and Self-Awareness.

Bibliography

Bargh, J. A., & Morsella, E. (2008). The Unconscious Mind. *Perspectives on Psychological Science*, *3*(1), 73–79. https://doi.org/10.1111/j.1745-6916.2008.00064.x
Beebe, L. H., & Wyatt, T. H. (2009). Guided imagery and music: Using the bonny method to evoke emotion and access the unconscious. *Journal of Psychosocial Nursing and Mental Health Services*, *47*(1), 29–33. https://doi.org/10.3928/02793695-20090101-02
Bento, R. F., & Nilsson, W. O. (2009). *(PDF) Visual Metaphors: A New Language for Discovery and Dialogue*. Teaching & Learning Journal. www.researchgate.net/publication/254967238_Visual_Metaphors_A_New_Language_for_Discovery_and_Dialogue
Dijksterhuis, A. (2004). Think different: The merits of unconscious thought in preference development and decision making. *Journal of Personality and Social Psychology*, *87*(5), 586–598. https://doi.org/10.1037/0022-3514.87.5.586
Domke, D., Perlmutter, D., & Spratt, M. (2002). The primes of our times? An examination of the "power" of visual images. *Journalism*, *3*(2), 131–159. https://doi.org/10.1177/146488490020 0300211
Elgendi, M., Kumar, P., Barbic, S., Howard, N., Abbott, D., & Cichocki, A. (2018). Subliminal priming—state of the art and future perspectives. *Behavioral Sciences*, *8*(6), 54. https://doi.org/10.3390/bs8060054
Gray, R. P. (2019). *Art Therapy and Psychology*. Routledge.
Heshmat, S. (2019). *Music, Emotion, and Well-Being | Psychology Today*. www.psychologytoday.com/us/blog/science-choice/201908/music-emotion-and-well-being
Jung, C. G., Henderson, J. L., Jacobi, J., Jaffé, A., & Franz, M.-L. vo. (1964). *Man and his Symbols* (C. G. Jung & M.-L. vo. Franz (eds.)). Aldus Books Ltd.
Kellermann, N. P. F. (2013). Epigenetic transmission of holocaust trauma: Can nightmares be inherited? *Israel Journal of Psychiatry and Related Sciences*, *50*(1), 33.

Lakoff, G. (2015, April 7) *How Brains Think: The Embodiment Hypothesis* [Keynote address]. International Convention of Psychological Science. www.youtube.com/watch?time_conti nue=102&v=WuUnMCq-ARQ

Lerner, J. S., Li, Y., Valdesolo, P., & Kassam, K. S. (2015). Emotion and decision making. *Annual Review of Psychology, 66*, 799–823. https://doi.org/10.1146/annurev-psych-010213-115043

Lubart, T. I. (2001). Models of the creative process: Past, present and future. *Creativity Research Journal, 13*(3–4), 295–308. https://doi.org/10.1207/s15326934crj1334_07

Minas, R. K., & Dennis, A. R. (2019). Visual Background Music: Creativity Support Systems with Priming. *Journal of Management Information Systems, 36*(1), 230–258. https://doi.org/10.1080/07421222.2018.1550559

Nisbett, R. (2017). The Incredible Shrinking Conscious Mind. *The Psychologist*, 36–37.

8 Symbolic Images and Visual Metaphors

Defining Symbols and Metaphors

Although a symbol and metaphor are two distinct things, they are also intricately linked, with symbols often employed in metaphors as a figure of speech. (For this reason, the term *symbolisation*, which refers to imbuing things with symbolic meaning, is also used in this chapter when referring to symbolic imagery and visual metaphors concurrently). This close relationship means how they are used and understood is not always clearly delineated.

Nevertheless, generally speaking, a *metaphor* is used to understand and experience one thing in terms of another (Lakoff & Johnson, 1980). For example, with the metaphor 'time is money,' money is a tangible object, time is abstract and personal. However, in relating the former to the latter, it takes on a physical quality that can be made sense of and explained to others in a way they will also understand. Money is considered a high-value commodity, and people rarely seem to have enough. It can be earned, wasted, and lost. The everyday language of "stop wasting time," "they spent time doing…," and "we've lost time on this" are metaphors that express the conceptualisation of time in terms of money.

A symbol stands for something else, referencing qualities inherent in the original object to create direct associations. In particular, when material objects represent abstract qualities. For example, an elephant might be a symbol of strength, community, and wisdom because it is associated with those attributes.

Throughout human history, symbols and metaphors have played an essential role in communication and meaning-making. Whether in business, science, and technology, or the arts, psychology, and philosophy, amongst others. However, they are often so embedded within community and national cultures that they are overlooked and taken for granted, without awareness that their role in creating meaning and connections, for and between us, remains as significant today as when the first ones emerged.

Their influence is rooted in the way brains look for patterns to process and understand new information, as to create meaning, new knowledge is related to what is already understood. This process is akin to putting a jigsaw puzzle together where individual pieces do not provide enough information to convey meaning. However, when linked to ones already positioned, they continue to build a picture that makes sense. Therefore, what was already known, becomes a vehicle through which comprehension and integration of

DOI: 10.4324/9781003017028-10

new learning occur. These associations find expression as symbols and metaphors, which may be individual, collective, verbal, visual or a combination. Even though metaphorical connections often appear incongruent, as creative and imaginative beings, humans have the remarkable capacity to make sense and create meaning where it is not immediately apparent. In addition to meaning-making through association with existing knowledge, a study in the field of psychoanalysis argues that metaphors inform and turn people towards the world of possibilities (Enckell, 2010). The argument is that as two subjects that do not belong together are nevertheless combined, different connections are created, and this elicits new meaning. Enckell describes these metaphors as enabling the birth of new knowledge, by raising awareness of a truth that has not yet arrived, a conscious awareness still to come. From the perspective of the CCT, both meaning-making and new knowledge are regularly observed as client outcomes. An example of these seemingly disparate connections is seen in the case study 'The Power of Personal Visual Metaphors' shared later in the chapter.

Symbols and Metaphors | The Theory

Symbols

As a pioneer of utilising the client's symbols in his work with them, Jung described a symbol as a word or picture that may be familiar in daily life but hold additional specific connotations to its original meaning (Jung et al., 1964). He characterises these symbolic images as having the capacity to express and embody what may be hard to articulate, providing emotional and spiritual meaning where words cannot. Because of this, they allow more complex and abstract ideas and emotions to be understood and conveyed. These symbols, emerging from the unconscious, are either deeply personal or universal as part of a society's collective unconscious (like the poppy for Remembrance Day). Jung believed the collective unconscious had primarily mythical and religious foundations. Although with many symbols, this is undoubtedly the case, it is worth remembering that Jung was writing before mass globalisation, widespread secularism, and the Internet. Consequently, where archetypal symbols indeed have roots in myths and religions, this connection is not always immediately apparent. Furthermore, just as language evolves, reflecting the continual shifts in societies and cultures, additional universal and cultural symbols have emerged over time from modern disciplines such as technology, neuroscience, and genetics (Enckell, 2010).

Metaphors

The seminal book "Metaphors We Live By" (Lakoff & Johnson, 1980) provides a comprehensive examination of the role of metaphor as a form of language that shapes communication, and accordingly, the way people think. The writers state that as thought processes are predominantly metaphorical, therefore, so is speech. This figurative language then serves as an external indication of internal conceptualisation. However, even though metaphorical language is an integral part of everyday dialogue, its complete integration within communication means its near-constant use goes unnoticed. Additionally, metaphors are more complicated than they first appear. Examples include the use of orientational ones, such as "I'm feeling down," or "She's really upbeat," where down is sad and happy is up, or container metaphors, such as 'holding the silence.' In writing about metaphorical language, Lakoff and Johnson drew attention to the importance of understanding its impact on thinking, and consequently, behaviour.

Embodiment

Arguably, the difference between symbols and metaphors is at times indiscernible, explaining why Lakoff (2012) refers to symbols as primary metaphors originating from repeated embodied experiences. Lakoff adds that wherever these repetitive experiences occur, they are usually cross-cultural. Essentially, opening a door, walking down a path, and other such events are actions familiar to everyone. Subsequently, leading to the symbolism of doors as transition and life as a journey, etcetera.[1] These examples typify the physicality of many metaphors, in that they reflect the characteristics and knowledge of bodily experiences (Lakoff & Johnson, 1980). Therefore, working with these symbolisations allows clients to access knowledge experienced through their bodies, providing alternative ways of processing information, gaining understanding, and increasing self-awareness. This form of learning is known as embodied cognition. Based on neuroscientific research, the premise is that mental processing is intrinsically linked to the body (Foglia & Wilson, 2017). This is significant when coaching with collage, as even in the absence of direct sensory input, embodiment enables clients to conceptualise often abstract ideas based on the memories of physical actions conveyed in their symbolisation (Foglia & Wilson, 2013).

Where embodiment is not experienced, the human imagination and mythology create the association instead. An example of this is a bird in flight or the transformation of a phoenix. While both are symbolisations, neither are embodied experiences.

The following reflection illustrates the concept of embodiment.[2]

Andréa's Personal Reflections | Key as Symbol

"One of my symbols is the key, and I am aware of the point at which it took on embodied symbolic meaning for me. In my early twenties, I purchased my first home for myself and my daughter. On the day of the move, I recall standing outside the front door, and my mum handing me the house keys. I was fully aware of the significance of what was happening, and I believe my mum was also. Like a rite of passage, I first unlocked and then opened the door to our new home, before stepping forward into it. Undoubtedly, because of its status as an archetype, the key as symbol already existed as part of my psyche. However, because I was not just opening any door, keys became embodied as a symbol of new opportunities, transition, independence, security, personal growth, and provision. My key symbol is also intrinsically linked to the metaphor of doors opening.

The symbol then lay dormant until it appeared in my first collage before founding UnglueYou®. With a theme of doors opening, it is unsurprising that it surfaced to remind me of everything it had stood for and what I needed to remember as I considered transitioning careers. Moreover, in exploring the symbol, I came to understand that I see myself as both a recipient and provider of keys, which manifests in many areas of my life, including coaching.

Keys continued to appear in my collages during the early years of my business. But it has since fallen into disuse because I implicitly know and trust that I have what they stand for, and therefore no longer need reminding. However, from experience, I know that it will surface in my collages again if needed. As Jung et al. (1964) assert, symbols surface from the unconscious to help address imbalances in the psyche."

Differentiating Symbols and Metaphors When Coaching with Collage

Symbols and metaphors present as both linguistic and visual forms of language. Regardless of the structure, they act as vehicles for meaning-making because the word(s) or image carry within them the associated concept. Therefore, there is an acceptance that whenever symbols and metaphors are engaged in coaching, the whole meaning is not immediately present (Enckell, 2010). Instead, they point to something else, providing scope for expansion and access to unseen materials, increased knowledge, and insight at multiple levels. These inherent qualities offer clients the opportunity to move closer to a complete sense of self, along with the chance to create deeper connections and collective understanding during group work.

In the Collage Coaching Technique™ (CCT), they first emerge for the client in a visual format, as symbolic images and visual metaphors. However, because symbols are employed within metaphorical language, an image may represent a symbol and metaphor simultaneously. Despite this potential for overlap, there are ways of differentiating a symbolic image from a visual metaphor on a client's collage. Visual metaphors are primarily influenced by external circumstances. Therefore, they are more susceptible to change, usually holding a temporary meaning that reflects the client's current psychological state. Consequently, the meaning attributed to the image may alter from one collage to the next. They are not part of the collective unconscious.

In contrast, with symbols, the personal meaning assigned to them remains consistent, regardless of the context or frequency of use. Although client symbols may fall into disuse over time or alternatives surface (reflecting their internal process of change), the original symbolic meaning does not change. The client's image may or may not be part of the collective unconscious. In summary, symbolic images refer to those that repeatedly have the same meaning, whereas visual metaphors describe images whose interpretation changes.

While visual metaphors are reliable indicators of how someone relates to themselves, others, and their current situation, personal symbolic images speak more to the core of who they are and can point to values, beliefs, and foundational truths.

Table 8.1.1 outlines these differences.

Table 8.1.1 Definition of symbols and metaphors in the CCT.

Personal Symbolic Images	Personal Visual Metaphors
Attributes assigned to the image remain consistent	Attributes assigned to the image may change
Meaning is static	Meaning is fluid
May be part of the collective unconscious	Not part of the collective unconscious
Relates to core values, beliefs, and foundational truths	Reflects relationship to self, others, and circumstances
Unaffected by changes to external circumstances	Alters according to changes to external circumstances

These descriptors are not definitive, they are a point of reference, and neither client nor coach should feel constrained by them.

Case Studies and Reflections | On Client Symbolisation

It is rare for clients to be aware of their symbolisations and, as such, recognise them immediately in their collage. Often, they decide to include an image without understanding why, their only knowledge lies in being certain they want it on their collage. This decision is intuitive knowledge that the client trusts, albeit unaware of the significance of the image until the connection emerges during the coaching conversation. Occasionally, symbolisations also surface via repetition of an image as shape, pattern, or form, either in one collage[3] or over a series. Regardless of how they present, these hitherto hidden and unfamiliar symbolisations typically provide the richest insights and breakthroughs for clients as they move from a place of uncertainty and indecision to clarity and focus. This discovery evolves through further, careful exploration and development of their image.[2]

Case Study | The Gradually Emerging Symbol

Clients may already be aware of their personal symbolic images and recognise them immediately in their collage. At other times, understanding occurs via repetition, either in one collage or over a series, as unfolded with this client.

Shelena created three collages using the CCT before becoming aware that an image was echoing across all three. An individual stood with their legs slightly apart, arms down, back straight, and shoulders square. They held their head up and held their gaze firmly forward. Although this character appeared in different guises, as a woman, an archetypal

Figure 8.1.1 Shelena's emergent symbol on leadership.

cowboy, and a swimmer who stood underwater, the stance remained the same. In the context of the rest of her collage and circumstances, Shelena previously explored each one as it surfaced. However, the symbolic significance of the figure was not apparent until it emerged a third time. With this new knowledge, Shelena shared as follows:

"The images represent strength, someone with a commanding stance who is steadfast. There is a leadership and signposting element to it that says, 'Look at me, I am strong.[2] Look!' I also have a sense of a call to action that says, 'You can do this; this is who you are even in extremes.' Each one is in a different place, and the one under the water really speaks to me. It says to me 'Your environment has no impact on your state.' With this knowledge, I have the strength, courage, and character to face challenges and overcome. This serves to give me strength, when I feel weak and unequipped, because these images remind me that my Spirit knows who I am, even when my soul and body sometimes forget, or is overwhelmed with the challenges of life. This encouraging insight has come at a very poignant time as I feel like I'm pivoting and finding out more about who I am as a leader and what I'm called to do." (Shelena)

These images are an external visual representation of the client's stages of transformation over time. Indicated firstly through the figure becoming more prominent as the back and foreground become less covered with each subsequent image. Secondly, by the third image, the swimmer (Shelena) is standing without the need for shielding or protection. There is no armour, as she first described the material surrounding the woman, neither is there a gun for defence, as with the cowboy.

Case Study | Symbolic Associations

There will be times when clients explain an image in literal terms. For example, "This image of a dog is here because I love dogs. They're so friendly, loyal, and great companions. They never ask anything of you. They don't let you down like people do." In these situations, clients are not immediately making a connection between themselves and the image beyond liking the object it portrays. Approaches to bridge this gap include, among others, Clean Language[4] and the gently probing questions, "Does that resonate with you on any level?". This enquiry allows client reflection concerning whether that may be the case, and if so, in what way. The question is deliberately phrased as a closed question and not asked, "How does it resonate with you?" because an open question assumes a degree of resonance when this is not always the case. If the response is in the affirmative, another layer of learning unfolds. In this case, the client responded, "I guess I see myself as being friendly and loyal. I get so upset when other people aren't the same." The association of dogs with those attributes allowed the image to emerge in symbol form. On further exploration, the client explained how it reflected his values concerning personal and professional relationships. To deepen his knowledge so he could better recognise what he sought in relationships, Clean Language was used to help him interpret and clarify how he understood, demonstrated, and experienced friendly and loyal.

Case Study | The Power of Personal Visual Metaphors

In 2013, Vicky, a psychologist who had not long started her coaching practice, contacted me for a consultation. She chose to work with me as her curiosity meant she wanted to discover more about the process after hearing it could be a valuable way to clarify values and unblock psychological obstacles. Vicky remarked, "Essentially, I wanted to find a way

Figure 8.1.2 Vicky's collage on self-belief and confidence.

to think through what was important to me and feel confident in owning my place as a coaching professional."

Among the images on Vicky's completed collage were two that helped her express, explore, and then reveal her truth concerning the internal thoughts she had concerning her skills, abilities, and confidence. Firstly, she spoke about how she experienced imposter syndrome, a psychological term relating to recurring feelings of self-doubt concerning achievements, coupled with the fear of getting found out as a fraud who does not know what they are doing. The image that reflected this for her was the caricature on the left. Here she described a (male) coach working in the corporate sector and charging a substantial fee. She could not relate to this version of a coach whose perceived way of working, dress, demeanour, and values did not align with hers. On reflection, she said, "It's entirely feasible that I thought I wouldn't be taken seriously if I didn't dress and present myself in an austere manner. Which I thought was required to be considered eligible to be an executive coach. It was not until later that I realised my authentic style serves me well." She had used the word 'fake' because that is how she felt at the time, unlike a 'real' coach compared to her peers.

Vicky had also used an image of a mixologist on her collage. She shared how she did not know why that image had resonated with her so profoundly but knew she had to include it in her collage. To assist Vicky in her interpretation of the image, I used Clean Language and asked, "And what kind of mixologist is he?" She replied:

"He's the kind of mixologist who has the training, skills and knowledge needed to create classic cocktails, but also, adds this to his experience and creativity to deliver new, innovative combinations based on customers' bespoke requests."

As she finished describing this image, Vicky had a conscious awareness that she was referring to herself through the mixologist as a metaphor. Like the mixologist, as an experienced trainer, coach, and psychologist, she also possessed a broad range of skills, knowledge, and creativity. When working with business clients, she could bring the best mix of these together to deliver solutions that met their specific requirements. Immediately after this, Vicky had an a-ha moment, as her tacit knowledge became elicit. In her feedback, she shared how she no longer felt like a fake and described herself as excited about her future.

"I have more clarity about what I bring to my profession and am able to articulate that better and believe it! I'm feeling more comfortable in acknowledging my 'stripes' and therefore more confident to share with others."

Six months later, Vicky messaged me with an update.

"I've certainly been feeling more like I earned my stripes since our session; it was great to reach that realisation. I'm sure that fed into my confidence to agree to be part of a new project via a company based in San Francisco. I provide remote performance coaching for emerging leaders. I'm loving the work I do with them." (Vicky)

The Role of Symbolisation in Creating Change

Without awareness of its powerful meaning, Vicky had intuitively wanted to include the image of the mixologist on her collage. As a personal visual metaphor, it had resonated deeply with her on an unconscious level, reflecting what she already knew internally. Despite this pre-existing knowledge, Vicky had either forgotten or no longer believed it due to imposter syndrome. Nonetheless, she had trusted her instinctive feeling and not discarded the image.

By surfacing her internal beliefs and feelings to a conscious level through the visual metaphor, it became possible to explore, assess, and review them during the coaching conversation. As she gained insight, clarity, and deeper self-awareness, Vicky understood and accepted the truth about her capabilities, skills, and knowledge. Accordingly, she developed a greater level of self-trust, empowering her to make a decision that moved her career forward with a sense of joy.

A client does not need to understand the difference between a symbolic image and a visual metaphor to experience personal development. Nonetheless, it is worthwhile raising awareness of their function and influence on beliefs and behaviours. Subsequently, clients can choose to own, redefine, or discard their existing symbols and metaphors. As new ones emerge with meanings that empower and promote their personal and professional growth, they have the option to accept these, rather than ones that reinforce limiting beliefs and prevent them from fulfilling their potential. Besides the role of uncovering meaning and bringing clarity, symbolisation also improves clients' ability to make decisions based on greater awareness of their qualities and values, as illustrated by Vicky's case study.

Avoiding Assumptions and Interpretations

Everyone has a unique symbolic and metaphorical language that is learnt and based on a combination of shared cultural experiences, beliefs, and individual lived experiences (Crick & Grushka, 2009). Each life lesson builds on a previous one, and connecting new information to existing knowledge creates a complex network of interrelated personal metaphors (Sullivan & Rees, 2008). Therefore, clients' symbolic images and visual metaphors have an infinite range of complex meanings, leaving them open to multiple interpretations, including the coach's. For this reason, working with symbolisation in coaching is never about interpreting clients' images, or making assumptions about their relationship with them.

The risk of projective interpretation increases when the coach has a strong personal connection to the image. Although trained not to follow a personal agenda, the meaning attributed to symbolisations can be felt so strongly in the psyche that coaches should remain alert to its potential impact on their practice. Without full awareness of the 'self' in the coaching space, projection can occur at an unconscious level, the one at which the symbol and metaphor originate. In these circumstances, the coaching conversation may unintentionally be influenced or steered in a direction believed to elicit client break-through. It is always preferable not to ask certain questions, or present information if there is any sense of such influence. This stance is imperative; otherwise, there is a risk of disempowering clients from taking responsibility for their self-development and ability to create change.

Coaches can avoid this outcome by remaining curious about the evolving nature of clients' images and mindful of their internal supervisor. The former involves trusting that clients will find their meaning and breakthrough, while the latter concerns the coach monitoring and responding to personal thoughts and emotional reactions.

Andréa's Personal Reflections | Listening to the Inner Supervisor

Example 1: Avoiding projection

During a group workshop, a client used the image of a squirrel in a bird feeder on his collage. While sharing his collage Emmanuel talked at length about the squirrel, which he saw as getting past the first barrier, described as "exceedingly tricky," only to face another, and now be stuck between them. He interpreted this visual metaphor as barriers put up

Figure 8.1.3 Photograph by Dwight Sipler on Flickr.

by others that prevented him from succeeding. Whereas, I saw it representing ingenuity as the squirrel had overcome the first barrier. I immediately recognised that my perspective was a result of projection as well as the well-meaning but misplaced desire to make things better for him by adopting the role of rescuer and sharing what I saw as a 'positive' perspective. However, I knew if I did I would deny Emmanuel the opportunity for discovery and ownership of the meaning. Equipped with this self-awareness, I knew not to ask a leading question, or propose an alternative view with the intention of steering him towards my interpretation. Instead, I focused on continuing to listen. After a while sharing his story, Emmanuel said, "If the squirrel got in, it can make its way out. As long as it stops to think and doesn't panic." When asked if this resonated with him on any level, he replied it related to being unemployed and dealing with government agencies he felt were preventing him from making any progress. He then expressed how as a man, the expectation was that he would not show his emotions but how hard this was for him adding, "I feel like my emotions are all caged up, and sometimes all I want to do is let them out because talking helps." Emmanuel stated how he also saw the squirrel as a reflection of this experience. In this way, the visual metaphor provided him with two meanings, both relating to the barriers he faced.

Example 2: Facilitating further exploration

The coach's perspective has the potential to add value to a client's self-discovery only when presented as a considered question occurring as part of an open coaching conversation. Applied on a case by case basis, a carefully constructed question affords the client an alternative way of viewing their image that may lead to further exploration, reflection, and knowledge, as in the following example.

Amy's coaching session was focused on what she wanted from her coaching practice. The digital collage she created included an image of upturned hands painted with henna which she described as open, giving, and helpful. I shared her interpretation of them as hands that could be giving and also saw them as receiving. Using Clean

Figure 8.1.4 Photograph by Ravi Sharma on Unsplash.

Language[4] I supported Amy in eliciting deeper meaning from her choice of words. Then, understanding my intention was to enable further exploration rather than steer her towards any particular insight, I asked her what it would be like to see the hands as receiving? Her response initiated further trains of thought around how she saw her coaching practice that proved valuable to her. Like with all clients, Amy had the choice to either disregard or explore the question depending on whether it connected with her. As the personal interpretation of images is strong, clients feel confident to discount the coach's question if there is no resonance.

Summarising Symbolisations

Whether personal or collective, symbols and metaphors play an integral role in communication and meaning-making. Their value lies in allowing abstract, complex, or emotional concepts to be conveyed and understood. When coaching with collage, these symbolisations manifest visually, facilitating access and connection to knowledge in a way that enables clients to view and evaluate their internal processing of experiences. Because of the deep connection and meaning these images evoke for both the client and coach, to avoid projection when working with clients and their symbolisations, coaches have a responsibility to monitor their internal dialogue and subsequent responses.

Bibliography

Crick, R. D., & Grushka, K. (2009). Signs, symbols and metaphor: linking self with text in inquiry-based learning. *The Curriculum Journal*, *20*(4), 447–464. https://doi.org/10.1080/0958517090 3425069

Enckell, H. (2010). Reflection in psychoanalysis: On symbols and metaphors. *International Journal of Psychoanalysis*, *91*(5), 1093–1114. https://doi.org/10.1111/j.1745-8315.2010.00320.x

Foglia, L., & Wilson, R. (2017). *Embodied Cognition, The Stanford Encyclopedia of Philosophy*. https://plato.stanford.edu/archives/spr2017/entries/embodied-cognition/.

Foglia, L., & Wilson, R. A. (2013). Embodied cognition. *Wiley Interdisciplinary Reviews: Cognitive Science*, *4*(3), 319–325. https://doi.org/10.1002/wcs.1226

Jung, C. G., Henderson, J. L., Jacobi, J., Jaffé, A., & Franz, M.-L. vo. (1964). *Man and his Symbols* (C. G. Jung & M.-L. vo. Franz (eds.)). Aldus Books Ltd.

Lakoff, G. (2012). Explaining Embodied Cognition Results. *Topics in Cognitive Science*, *4*(4), 773–785. https://doi.org/10.1111/j.1756-8765.2012.01222.x

Lakoff, G., & Johnson, M. (1980). *Metaphors We Live By*. University of Chicago Press.

Sullivan, W., & Rees, J. (2008). *Clean language, Revealing Metaphors and Opening Minds*. Crown House Publishing Ltd.

PART 2 | CLEAN LANGUAGE AND THE COACHING CONVERSATION

Because the inherent nature of symbolic images and visual metaphors conveys more than what is seen on the surface, they must undergo a process of meaning-making led by the client and supported by the coach. The first stage in this process begins as clients construct their collage,[5] facilitating reflection, analysis, and evaluation. Symbolic and metaphorical meaning is usually understood intuitively. However, as the next step involves sharing their visual narrative, to enable coherent telling, clients start to order and construct their thoughts which stimulates further comprehension. Then, as a form of exploration, the coaching conversation allows clients to evolve, deepen, and consolidate their symbolisations' meaning.

Clean Language

Just as art therapy is not about interpreting a client's images, the same is true in coaching. Instead, the aim is to work in a way that honours and trusts individuals' resonance to their symbolisations. As such, the coach's role is to work alongside the client, enabling them to voice their experiences, discover meaning that elicits personal knowledge, and increase their self-awareness. Accordingly, the coaching conversation must allow information to emerge into the client's conscious awareness from exploring and interpreting their symbolic images and visual metaphors. The Clean Language technique is ideally suited to this approach because of its focus on removing assumptions and external influences from the questioning.

The counselling psychologist, David Grove, developed Clean Language in the 1980s while working with trauma patients. He noticed that the most effective method for releasing them from the effects of the trauma was by asking patients to use metaphors to describe their feelings (Wilson, 2004). A style of questions was developed to reduce contamination due to questioner biases and interpretations, thereby "…freeing up the resources of the person being questioned so that they can think effectively for themselves" (Sullivan & Rees, 2008, p. 10). The practitioners, Penny Tompkins and James Lawley have since advanced the technique, intending to make it more accessible. Their methodology, known as Symbolic Modelling, organises the initial questions developed by Grove into a set of 12 developing questions.

Exploring Language | Understanding Personal Definitions

Within the coaching conversation, the CCT utilises two from the set of 12 'Developing questions.' These are:

1   and what kind of [x] is that?[6]
2   and is there anything else about [x]?

As a form of personal storytelling, when clients share their collage, the language tends to be highly descriptive, vivid, expressive, and emotive. These evocative words carry extensive meaning. However, the client may not be completely aware of what it suggests for them personally. Although not obviously metaphorical, interpretation of language such as "safe," "strong," or "free" carry different associations for individuals based on factors that include culture, demographics, upbringing, and life experiences. Therefore, when discussing their images, it is imperative to support clients to clarify the qualities and associated behaviours of the words used to describe these profoundly personal symbolisations.

The question "And what kind of 'safe' is that?" compels them to pause and deliberate on specific words. This mode of inquiry provides the method to elicit the clarity of language that supports meaning-making by removing ambiguity. Additional benefits with this type of approach are:

- minimising the risk that clients' understanding is based on societal norms and expectations rather than their values and perceptions
- removing assumptions based on the coach's interpretation

There is an appreciation that sometimes the client's first response may be, "I don't know." However, given the time and space[7] they are capable of elaborating. Coach's must also accept that the nature of metaphors mean that client understanding may not always come within the coaching session.

Once the client answers, the coach repeats the "what kind of?" question in response to the language that emerges. By continuing to dialogue in this way the coach facilitates clients' continued exploration of their sense of the word. The question "And is there anything else about [x]?" supports this process through an opportunity for final reflection and awareness of reaching completion at a particular point, or of a specific subject. For this reason, it is always used immediately after a client finishes sharing their collage, phrased as "and is there anything else about the collage?" Other examples include:

- and is there anything else about strong?
- and is there anything else about this image?

From the coach's perspective, the Clean Language[8] technique can initially feel awkward, unnatural, and even repetitive. However, for the client, while with the coach it affords them a chance to reach the potential of their meaning-making, accepting that this process continues outside of the coaching environment. Overall, the technique is advantageous because as clients seek the words to articulate answers to the questions, they continually expand their use of descriptive or metaphorical language. Consequently, they capture the core meaning evoked by the visuals in their collage and access the wealth of knowledge, information, and intuitive guidance contained in their symbolisations.

The following two examples of exploring the word 'strong' serve to illustrate the importance of clarifying a client's personal meaning of their metaphorical language.

Case Study #1 | Shelena's Exploration of the Word 'Strong'

This dialogue took place following recognition of the connection between the three figures in Shelena's collages.[9] (See Figure 8.1.1)

ANDRÉA: Strong, that was one of the words you used to describe your images, and what kind of strong is that?

SHELENA: I think that's internal strong. I'm not talking about physical strength; it's definitely an internal strength. I'm thinking of strength of leadership and mind, strength of resolve, regardless of the environment.

ANDRÉA: So strength of leadership, mind, and strength of resolve. When you use the word leadership, what kind of leadership is that?

SHELENA: I mean, everybody's a leader, aren't they? Everybody's leading someone, even if it is just themselves. But I've known for a while that people will follow me, so for me, I guess that means you're a leader, and so it's strength in that knowledge. In this current environment, the implications of weak leadership are very clear. We rise or fall on strong leadership, and in these pictures, I see strong leadership with very clear resolve and that they can take the knocks.

ANDRÉA: You've described strong leadership as being resolved, very clear, and they can take the knocks. Anything else about strong leadership?

(A period of silence)

SHELENA: I think maybe having that vision for where you're taking people. It doesn't mean everything is exactly clear, but like having a blueprint of where you're going and being able to communicate that, take it forward and bring people with you.

ANDRÉA: Does that resonate with you?

SHELENA: It just helps me to reflect on my own leadership and my leadership style, and it makes me think about what I feel is impacting on my leadership, where I need to develop really.

ANDRÉA: And do you know where you need to develop?

SHELENA: I've got some ideas. I think we're actually powerless in certain things, so recognising where my leadership starts and ends. I can't push things on like I want to. I have to accept there's limitations to my leadership and respond accordingly.

ANDRÉA: And is there anything else about strong leadership

SHELENA: I don't think so.

(A period of silence)

ANDRÉA: And what will you do with what you know now?

SHELENA: I love leadership, I think that one of my passions is great leaders, I love to watch them, they're so inspiring. I want to search someone out to learn from them and receive mentoring or coaching.

In this example the question "and what kind of?" was also used for resolve, knocks and other metaphorical language that came out of the leadership discussion. However, for emphasis the conversation has been condensed.

Case Study #2 | Rosie's Exploration of the Word 'Strong'

In the discussion below, Rosie is referring to the image of the woman on a swing positioned at the top of her collage. (See Figure 14.1)

ROSIE: I swing myself free. I like that affirmation. I like that her hair is just in the air and when she's doing it, she's strong. I mean, she's having fun of course, but you cannot be on a swing and just be loose. You need to be firm and strong, otherwise you fall. She looks like she has some sort of presence, you know and looking at the sun, the background it's also very beautiful. This is like a gentle afternoon enjoyment, she seems to be looking and moving forward, so there is a strength there to move forward.

ANDRÉA: You've used the image as an affirmation. You like that her hair's out behind her, and to swing you need to be strong and firm. You also mentioned that she looks like she's got a presence, is going forward and has the strength to do that. So I want to start by asking you, when you say strong, what kind of strong is that?

ROSIE: Swinging used to be my favourite thing when growing up, and then I just stopped. I remember you have to push yourself, I mean, it's nice when you're doing a little bit, but it's also nice when you are pushing yourself.

(A period of silence)

I would say decisive, because the decision to swing doesn't just happen. I can have the decision, but nothing happens if I don't put it into action. So I'm going very high, super high, because I want to see how high I can go and I don't want to lose. If I'm going to do that, I actually have to put a lot of effort in, because it's basically following the decision that I'm going to go quite high. And okay, I'm also going to bear the internal, because when I'm doing that my body feels it, and I don't know if I would be able to do it now, because now I feel it more, if that makes sense. So yes, I guess it's the mindset of being on the swing, being strong and wanting something and putting in all the effort to get it.

Explorative Conversation Techniques

Along with the Clean Language questions, there are three other core types of querying techniques employed in the CCT:

Table 8.2.1 Overview of Explorative Conversation Techniques Used in the CCT

Explorative Technique	Description	Example	Category
CLEAN LANGUAGE	Enquiry that works with a client's metaphorical language to bring clarity without adding external bias	• And what kind of [x] is that? • And is there anything else about [x]?	**Questions** Used to enhance meaning-making by bringing information and insights into the client's cognitive awareness via reflection and evaluation
DESCRIPTOR	Questions to help clients ascertain their goals by describing how they want to affect practical, emotional, mental, spiritual, or physical change.	Using the client's metaphorical/ descriptive language to frame the query. E.g., What is happening when you are strong?	
STATEMENT	Comments that elicit more information. (This approach is particularly helpful when clients use minimal words to share an image).	Describe what you see	**Comments** Facilitate further exploration and discovery. They also offer alternative approaches if clients find the questions challenging and struggle to answer them during the coaching conversation[4]
NOTICING	Fact-based observations (**not** subjective opinion or interpretation of images)	I notice the figures in your last three collages have a similar stance.	

- descriptors
- statements
- noticing

The four methods are grouped as two categories, 'Questions' and 'Comments.' The table 8.2.1 provides an overview of the techniques and is ordered according to the sequence of use during the coaching conversation.

While not a complete list of questions to ask within each category, this overview serves as a guide to structuring the coaching conversation. As coaches work with the CCT, there is also an expectation that they will see opportunities to draw on their existing tools, approaches, and skills as they follow its core guidance.

Bibliography

Sullivan, W., & Rees, J. (2008). *Clean Language, Revealing Metaphors and Opening Minds.* Crown House Publishing Ltd.

Wilson, C. (2004). *Metaphor & Symbolic Modelling For Coaches.* https://cleanlanguage.co.uk/articles/articles/89/1/Metaphor--Symbolic-Modelling-For-Coaches/Page1.html

PART 3 | ARCHETYPAL SYMBOLS

Archetypal images are instinctive, emerging from the psyche's collective unconscious, that part of the mind where humans share a universal ancestral memory and experience (Jung et al., 1964). The complexity of societies, cultures, and personal experience means that no individual symbolic image has a fixed representation. Yet, it is clear from different fields and research that humans still share similar symbols and metaphors as evidenced by clients' recurrent use of similar images in their collage to convey the same meaning. This connection is particularly prevalent where language and culture are shared (Crick & Grushka, 2009).

Collective Unconscious

Unlike personal symbols, being part of the collective, shared ones are more readily identifiable. The value in shared symbolic images is in combining the knowledge of the collective with an individual's interpretation, perspective, and meaning-making present in the picture. In essence, while the archetype offers clients a generic understanding, the specifics of the image reflect the client's personal experiences, emotions, and understanding. A door is a classic example. As an archetypal symbol of transition there remain significant differences between those that resonate with clients, whether relating to size, material, condition, or positioning. Even where the door is identical,[10] clients still interpret it according to their unique perspective. These variations allow exploration that leads to insight concerning how the client is experiencing the transitional process. This identification of personal understanding alongside the collective enables clients to gain a more meaningful connection to the symbol. As a result, some clients add it as a physical object within their environment. Examples include a crown, circular objects, crosses, water, and the colour green.

Understanding Archetypes

Assumptions cannot be made concerning what archetypes represent for clients and it is not the role of the coach to interpret their images. However, it remains beneficial for coaches to have a rudimentary knowledge of archetypal symbols because:

1   When clients describe their image only from the collective perspective, the coach recognises an opportunity for further exploration to facilitate personal meaning-making for them.
2   Symbols often co-exist on a collage. Therefore, clients may overlook some connections and patterns. Objective noticing statements bring these to their attention for exploration.
3. Clients may be curious regarding the archetypal meaning associated with their symbol. The time to offer this information comes when the client enquires or when the coaching conversation suggests this information will enhance the client's discovery and learning.

Many years of clients' comments and reactions have led me to conclude that in expressing an aspect of themselves that is rooted in the collective, clients experience a sense of universal knowledge. They describe this understanding that transcends the individual as significant and valuable, leading to an appreciation of their connection to others.

Redressing Imbalances

Nature per sé is not considered an archetypal symbol (elements are). Yet, the prevalence of images of the natural environment in clients' collages, regardless of the theme, evidences another fundamental human connection.

This occurrence may be explained by de Botton & Armstrong (2013) who propose people are drawn to artwork that fills a psychological gap and promises inner wholeness. For example, in this context, they state that as nature gradually vanishes from human life as a direct experience, it emerges in the arts through poetry and paintings. Individuals are then unconsciously drawn to these works because they restore within them a sense of equilibrium. Therefore, images of nature may resonate with clients as a way of redressing its absence. Invariably they express a desire to spend more time in this space, recognising they have an unfulfilled need that the natural environment satisfies. Clients consistently interpret these images as representing simplicity, stillness, relaxation, and peace. By reflecting this as a universal experience, images that depict nature are essentially archetypal and, like all symbolisation, emerge from the intuitive unconscious to guide clients to a sense of completeness, deeper connection to self, and fulfilment.

Archetypal Symbols

The following archetypal symbols frequently appear in clients' collages. As part of the collective unconscious many will be familiar and hold resonance for the reader. Each symbol's generic interpretation is shared, along with guidance to support clients' meaning-making. As symbols do not exist in isolation, what they reveal should always be explored in the context of all that the client presents.

Bird in Flight

Wings outstretched, soaring, seemingly without effort, the bird in flight is the most frequently occurring symbol used in collages. Its meaning is nearly always associated with a sense of boundless freedom, embodied in recognition of knowing how it feels to have arms outstretched, emulating a bird's wings. Flying birds are rooted in the desire for change, with a sense of soaring to new heights and improved circumstances by leaving problems behind. This connection to change is along similar lines to that of the door and

Figure 8.3.1 Photograph by TheOtherKev from Pixabay.

butterfly. The prevalence of its use in the context of coaching with the CCT points to the human need to live and express freely.

Perhaps this is why the symbol of the bird in flight is also likely to cause emotional overwhelm. As once clients begin sharing where they seek freedom, the sense of captivity or entrapment is brought starkly to conscious awareness. In group work, it is the symbol where others readily connect with the storyteller, understanding the deep sense of longing, even when the freedom they seek is different. As an abstract concept, freedom is highly individual, as such clients have described it as meaning release from perfectionism, judgement, anger, unforgiveness, shame, and failure. Other times, it is an actual desire to 'fly away' and leave behind a difficult personal or professional situation. It also concerns ill health, relationships, regrets, and careers. Regardless of what this freedom represents, the bird in flight surfaces to remind the client to 'spread their wings.'

Other less common symbols of freedom include arms outstretched, hot air balloons, and swings.

Questions to elicit deeper personal meaning for clients:

* what type of bird is it?
* what colour is it?
* what size is it?
* is it taking off, landing or in flight?

According to "The Book of Symbols" Carlson et al. (2010), both the bird and butterfly[11] refer to the soul.

Butterfly

Despite its fragility and short lifespan, the image of the butterfly captures the symbol of personal transformation. This meaning is connected to the nature of its life cycle, particularly the change from caterpillar to chrysalis and finally a butterfly. Through this metamorphosis, the act of transformation is at its most extraordinary and captivating. It is no wonder then, that when an individual desires to change something about their life, their unconscious often looks to the symbol of the butterfly.

Figure 8.3.2 Artwork by Georgire M Art at www.georgiem.art.

From the outset, the caterpillar has everything in its genetic make-up to become a butterfly. As a caterpillar, it must eat voraciously and while it grows sheds its skin several times before entering the chrysalis stage. During this transition there is no external indication that there is an internal process of genetic change occurring. Finally, as it emerges, it must expel the accumulated waste from the chrysalis stage and pump blood into its wings before it can take flight.

The use of this symbol holds more than the hope of change for the client. Because, if they are not already aware, it can also serve to connect them to the nature of transitions and the cycle of change. By sharing the details of the butterfly's transformational process it becomes a metaphor. Representing that, like the caterpillar, clients already possess all the core attributes and characteristics necessary to fulfil their potential and live a full, rich life. However, developing these is a process that takes time, work, struggle, stillness, patience, trust, and letting go of things that no longer serve them well.

Questions to elicit deeper personal meaning for clients:

- what colour is the butterfly?
- is it in flight or at rest?
- how many are there?

Door

The door or gate stands open, is firmly shut or sometimes slightly ajar. Whenever this entry and exit point appear they represent a point of transition, whether leaving something behind or entering a new state. Clients sometimes refer to this as closing the door on a chapter of their life. This symbolic connection with doors occurs because, in a literal sense, it is understood that going through a door means moving from one place to another. They are physical barriers separating different spaces, and their presence indicates that things are different on the other side. According to Carlson et al. (2010), in psychological terms, the door or gate is found between the inner and outer world.

The doors come in all shapes, sizes, materials, and positions. Sometimes light filters through as they stand ajar, combining two symbolic references. On occasion, they are closed, blocked, or locked and what is on the other side remains unknown. Gates however, which usually allow seeing what is beyond, emerge from the unconscious less frequently

Figure 8.3.3 Photograph by Andréa Watts.

than doors. The symbol of the door as a transition point, or at least an opportunity for one, may relate to any number of changes including careers, relationships, health, or psychological shifts in mental models. In this context, doors often represent opportunities. As expressed in the phrase "as one door closes, another one opens." Because doors are akin to passageways, they are also used to refer to moving through challenges or periods of emotional difficulty, such as anger, sadness, or guilt.

Questions to elicit deeper personal meaning for clients:

- what is the size, colour, material(s)?
- where is it positioned in the door frame – open, ajar, closed, blocked?
- is there any indication on the image of what is beyond the door or gate?
- is it part of a wider composition, for example, is it in a room or free-standing?
- which side of the door do they see themselves?

Road or Path

> The path is clear or so it seems,
> It opens up towards your dreams,
> But as you journey steadily on,
> It closes in and the way is gone.
> Look again and you will know,
> The true path lies within your soul,
> Follow this and you will find,
> Your heart's desire and peace of mind.
> *Andréa Watts*

"In essence, 'path' implies direction" (Carlson et al., 2010, p. 454). This meaning is inextricably connected to the metaphor 'life is a journey,' with its corresponding literal, and therefore visual representations, such as signposts, junctions, roadworks, and stop signs.

The symbolic imagery relating to the path as a 'direction in life's journey' emerges from the unconscious in an array of visual interpretations, reflecting the diversity of individuals' lived experiences and future direction of travel. Therefore, although the meaning is essentially the same, the path may surface for clients as a mountain pass, tunnel, stepping-stones,

Figure 8.3.4 Photograph by Larisa Koshkina from Pixabay.

woodland trail, road, railway track, or the like. Each image will also include further distinguishing features, such as being straight, meandering, wide, narrow, unobstructed, blocked, or any combination of these.

Additionally, knowing what it is to journey, the metaphor pervades verbal and visual language, with examples including:

- I'm at a crossroads – the image of a junction
- I feel directionless – multiple signs pointing different directions
- I've lost my way, or I want to carve my own path – woodland
- I want to expand my horizons – someone looking out at a landscape

The path as a symbolic image combines the client's metaphorical and embodied knowledge, helping them to understand their perception of their current situation or future. Consequently, as they explore this symbol, it offers insights and awareness to make informed decisions concerning their next steps. Reflection on the image, with interrelated ones present on the collage, serves to deepen personal discovery.

Client Reflections | On a Mountain Path and Career

"The image of the mountain reminds me of my recent walking holiday. I was determined to walk this trail and trained for months. As I couldn't find anyone to go with me, I went alone. Because it was isolated, it was incredibly quiet, and at times I wished there was someone with me. But the view was breath-taking, and I loved the stillness. This scene represents where I have reached so far in business. I recognise that I have worked hard to get where I am and have often gone it alone, which can feel lonely. Reflecting on how peaceful it felt up in the mountains and the wonderful views, I know it was worth the struggle to get where I am. Now it's okay to take a moment to reflect on and enjoy what I've accomplished, before pushing ahead to the next thing." (Jonathon)

This reflection demonstrates how the client drew on his embodied experience of preparing for and walking the mountain trail, his business development, and the path as a symbolic journey to decide his next steps. Consequently, he recognised that pausing and reflecting should be his priority.

The path is also a symbol for the inner spiritual journey, sometimes described as the path to enlightenment. Many spiritual practices and faiths believe in the concept of a right or wrong path, with Buddhism advocating a middle way. Linguistically, verbal metaphors also reveal this, with phrases such as "on the right track" or "they've lost their way."

The range of life's interrelated journeys, such as the emotional, physical, spiritual, and psychological, find symbolic expression, through the images of paths or roads that can guide clients to discover the right 'way' for them.

Questions to elicit deeper personal meaning for clients:

- is the path related to other images on the collage? are there other journey visuals?
- what kind of path or road is it? natural, constructed, and so forth?
- where does it lead?
- is there a sense of embodiment? if so, is this real, or perceived through visualisation and imagination?
- listen for the verbal journey metaphors, use clean language to discuss these

Figure 8.3.5 Photograph by Leandro De Carvalho from Pixabay.

Mask

In hiding the image of the true self, the role of the mask is to obscure identity and create another persona. From the earliest traditions, the belief was that the mask wearer embodied the characteristics it represented. Primarily connected to the domains of theatre and storytelling, mask-wearing evolved from rituals, worship, healing, and rites of passage. Later they became synonymous with masquerade balls, where they allowed wearers to act freely and out of character by conferring anonymity.

On a purely practical level, they function as a form of protection; examples include beaked masks worn by plague doctors, gas, and surgical masks. As a symbolic image, these references permeate the psyche, so that on occasions they surface to represent protection. However, predominantly, clients refer to 'wearing a mask' in terms of hiding their true self, seeking the confidence to remove it and live authentically.

Besides the familiar archetypal mask, it can emerge from the unconscious as a form of covering or obstruction that distorts or conceals the face or entire figure.

Usually, a single mask appears in the collage, yet clients may speak of multiple ones they wear trying to 'fit in,' recognising that they feel a pressure to conform to societal norms and external, or at times self-imposed expectations. Predominantly, the meaning relates to loss of identity. However, it is worth noting that masks do not always carry a negative connotation. Besides protection, they may also reflect a genuine part of the client's personality they have yet to express. Whichever it may be, in revealing itself visually, clients can identify the nature of the mask and begin the process of exploring its meaning.

Alternative imagery linked to the mask, what I refer to as the 'partial mask,' is symbolised by a figure with its hand, or something external, covering its mouth. In this instance, the most common interpretation is, "not having my voice heard."

Questions to elicit deeper personal meaning for clients:

- What type of mask is it? Archetypal, covering, obstruction, partial?
- What form does it take? Human, animal, mythical, other?
- Does it have defining characteristics?
- What is its purpose? Concealing 'self', protection, or undiscovered personality trait?

Figure 8.3.6 Photograph by niko photos on Unsplash.

Tree

As a cross-cultural and global icon, the tree transcends all people, faiths, and spiritual practices to offer symbolic resonance related to each of its parts and inherent qualities. With interconnected root systems that reach deep into the earth and branches that stretch to the skies, the tree is synonymous with resilience, remaining firmly planted and holding its ground through all weathers and the changing seasons. Accordingly, the word 'strong' is one of the adjectives most often used when describing the image of a tree.

Akin to water, trees engender a sense of providing solace, rest, and peace as well as shade and safety. These embodied experiences emerge as the client shares memories of time spent in the company of trees. Furthermore, images of trees are often associated with the familiar quote, "Mighty oaks from little acorns grow." This connection affirms that just as the small acorn slowly evolves into a large, resilient, majestic, and deep-rooted tree, it is possible to achieve great things from small beginnings. Psychologically, this unfolding takes place through little nudges of self, brought into conscious awareness that bud and grow (Carlson et al., 2010). By remaining steadfast through periods of growth and transformation, clients are better able to achieve their aspirations. For this reason, the image of the tree is a powerful archetype when included in a collage.

It is not possible to cover the breadth of symbolic references related to trees. However, a client's memories and how they relate to trees will provide opportunities for personal interpretation, meaning-making, and relevant insights.

Questions to elicit deeper personal meaning for clients:

- where is it?
- what season is it?
- what is the condition of the tree?
- is it solitary?
- what species is the tree?

Water

Water is one the elementals and most frequently emerges from the unconscious as vast expanses in the form of lakes and seas. Other water images that surface include rivers,

Figure 8.3.7 Photograph by Rony Michaud from Pixabay.

rain, waterfalls, ponds, and even showers. With its strong ties to religious symbolism, including baptism, it is often described by clients in the context of cleansing, purifying, and washing away. At the same time, the reflective qualities of water speak of looking back or within.

As an embodied symbol, clients repeatedly refer to this image as engendering a sense of peace and tranquillity; recalling memories of times spent on a quiet beach, by a calm lake or large pond, looking at the water in contemplation and reflection.

Conversely, it is also associated with drowning, literally and figuratively, with the sense of fear at 'being out of one's depth.' This phrase usually relates to water as a representation of overwhelm and associated emotions. Images of storms and large waves hold similar meaning, with clients describing a sense of anxiety and threat from external forces.

Questions to elicit deeper personal meaning for clients:

- what form does the water take?
- what is its condition? is it clean, dirty, other?
- if it is a body of water, is there anything floating on it?

Light

Light allows what could otherwise be obscured or hidden to be revealed or remain in view. It does this practically, figuratively, and psychologically. This is seen in the use of metaphorical language about reaching deeper understanding, such as "shedding light on a subject" or "having a light bulb moment." In a literal sense, it is understood that turning on a light illuminates the environment. This quality is frequently reflected in clients' chosen imagery, where rather than the light source being the subject matter, it brightens another feature in the image. Examples of this include sun rays through trees, windows, and creeping over mountain tops, or an image that is bright with no identifiable source of light. It may be obvious or subtle, natural or artificial, and when the subject matter is the client's focus, it may even seem incidental. In these instances, until drawn to their attention, the light is often initially overlooked.

Because the sun is the primary source of light on earth, symbolically it is also associated with the attributes of warmth, joy, and pleasure. As a result, light is considered

Figure 8.3.8 Photograph by Andréa Watts.

and experienced as virtuous, positive, pure, and uplifting. Familiar metaphoric language, including "they have been a ray of light" or "there is light at the end of the tunnel" encapsulate this meaning. From a spiritual perspective, light has an enduring association with newness, hope, cleansing, and healing.

Although darkness is the absence of light, so theoretically its opposite, representations of 'darkness' such as shadows, rarely appear on clients' collages. Instead, what they find psychologically challenging or emotionally uncomfortable, tends to surface through imagery that points to the problem.

Questions to elicit deeper personal meaning for clients:

- what is the source of the light?
- how much is there?
- where is it positioned relative to the subject?
- what is the subject matter of the image?

Fire

Another of the elementals, fire, is both a force for destruction and creation. A duality perfectly captured in the mythology of the phoenix, rising out of the ashes, transformed. This cyclical regeneration by fire is not merely mythological. In nature, there are places where fire destroys growth above ground, and as a result, stimulates seed dispersal for plants reliant on the fire to end their period of dormancy. Clients who gather images of raging fires, tap into this metaphor, describing the image as representing pain and trials alongside cleansing and transformation. They often recall the story of the phoenix, with a sense of hope and understanding that what may seem harmful at first, can prove a benefit long term.

In its guise as both friend and foe, fire captures the human imagination, from the dragon's breath to gods of mythology and religion. In Hinduism fire is seen as a deity, in Christianity an indwelling spirit, first appearing as flames above the disciples. Fire also illuminates the darkness, and therefore, is interchangeable with the symbol of light. In this context, the image clients tend to gather is that of lit candles, while making strong connections to hope, faith and persistence.

Figure 8.3.9 Photograph by István Asztalos from Pixabay.

Other recurring fire themes relate to fireplaces and campfires. Since humanity learnt how to control fire, it has been associated with providing warmth, protection, and food preparation. Unsurprisingly then, when sharing these images clients use adjectives such as warming, peaceful, comforting, and safe, often accompanied by a shift to a more relaxed tone and physiology. As an element of opposites, fire also speaks to clients of passion, energy, desire, anger, and hatred. Here related images of the sun, sparks, lava, and fireworks have also emerged to portray this range of fiery emotions.

Deeply ingrained in mythology, religion, language, and everyday life when fire arises from the unconscious, it holds multiple potential meanings for exploration.

Questions to elicit deeper personal meaning for clients:

- what kind of fire is it?
- where is it occurring?
- are there religious or mythological interpretations?
- what is its purpose? For example, destructive, creation, warming, protecting?

Client Reflections | On the Circle as an Archetypal and Personal Symbol

The circle is another universal symbol that repeatedly appears in collages. With no beginning or end, its shape elevates its meaning to that of totality, eternity, a status of wholeness, and in some religions, enlightenment. All interpretations relate to the circle as representing perfection and a sense of completion, with Dr Von Franz describing it as expressing "the totality of the psyche…including the relationship between man and nature" (Jung et al., 1964, p. 240).

The following reflection illustrates a client's symbolic experience of circles. The dialogue is a part of a larger conversation concerning her collage. Circles appeared multiple times in Joanne's collage as mirrors, clocks, plates, chair seats, bowls, a bicycle wheel, and other objects. While she understands it as an archetype, her thoughts express her interpretative meaning when she created the collage and in retrospect.

"I chose to work with Andréa because, at that time, I really struggled to get my voice and my words out, but I enjoyed being creative. When I created my collage, there was a lot

Image 8.3.10 Joanne's collage.

of non-acceptance and uncertainty over myself. The collage allowed me to see and under-stand myself, having those circles, the reflecting and being okay with that. Looking back, I was a very head person, which had the potential to get in the way and maybe give me distorted guidance. As part of my personal development, it was the beginning of finding my voice by allowing my unconscious to come through. So, I could allow what I needed to surface and then work with what arrived and I think, in fact I know, that's how I've continued working. But when I use the word 'think' it's not the cognitive thinking, it's the wider knowing and understanding of the whole, like the circle.

In terms of the symbolism of the circles, I see me as a hub. So, when I look at the bicycle wheel with all its spokes, the hub at the centre is me. Then all the spokes going off are different parts of myself, so it's about the whole of me and embracing all those elements that sit within the circle of me, to create this beautiful person that is central to herself. We also talk about the circle of life, but I follow the seasons, which is another form of circle. I also belong to a drum circle, that's my group and that circle is about my tribe.

The other thing about a circle, is there is no place to hide, but it also means everybody's equal. If you're in that circle or space, everyone is equidistant from the centre point. There's no hierarchy as part of that group, which relates to me on a personal level as it allows me to know that no one personal thing I try to work with has priority over the rest. At times, some might require a little bit more of my attention and focus, but it allows others to ebb and flow as they need to.

When I created the collage, the circles and mirrors probably came up unconsciously. But as I've grown, I've understood more about mirrors than in the sense of physical ones.

I can now see how they appear in my life, recognising, for example, that interaction with someone else can be a mirror that enables me to see something else of myself and have a different understanding. All the mirrors and the circles offer that light, that ability to reflect an image and see a different thing. But they don't tell you what's right or wrong, they just enable you to see without anyone saying what you have to do, or how you have to be. This enables me to make decisions, to see what I see and reflect upon it and work with it from there. That's really quite important for me.

I like the combination of concave and convex mirrors all together on the left side of the collage, because they give those different refractions of light, as well as reflecting the image. This allows you to understand that sometimes the view we have might be distorted. But by exploring and working with it, you're able to be open to what you see in front of you. I know that sometimes I may not have liked what I saw in the mirror because I didn't like myself, I couldn't say that I loved myself and things like that. So, to look in the mirror was really quite painful because of what was being reflected, compared to my perception about how I wanted things to be. One of the many little elements that were flagging through the collage.

When I look at it now and some of the reflections I've shared, they wouldn't necessarily have been reflections that I'd have had when I made it, because of the different experiences that have come along since. So, I want to share the power of looking back and reflecting further, because I can see that this collage still has massive place and purpose in my life and for me, it will always enable empowerment." (Joanne Fletcher)

Essentially, archetypal symbols offer an opportunity to access collective knowledge in combination with personal interpretation. This connection generates layers of learning for clients as they explore and draw on universal shared human experiences and understanding, alongside their individual meaning-making. In so doing, clients develop a more profound, meaningful connection beyond the generic to a unique relationship with the archetypal images that surface through their collages.

Notes

1 See Chapter 8 | Part 3: Archetypal Symbols.
2 See also Rosie's 'Exploration of the Word Strong' in chapter 8 part 3, and Trinity's reflections in chapter 10 part 1.
3 See Chapter 8 | Part 3: Archetypal Symbols (Client Reflections).
4 See Chapter 8 | Part 2: Clean Language and the Coaching Conversation.
5 See Chapter 9 | Creativity: Parts 2 & 3.
6 It is not always necessary to include the word 'and' when coaching with collage.
7 See Chapter 12 | Holding the Silence.
8 Clean Language becomes more natural with practice and courses are readily available to learn this coaching technique.
9 This case study is a continuation from Chapter 8 | Part 1: Shelena - The Gradually Emerging Symbol).
10 While this is rare when using magazines in the offline version of the CCT, it does occur. Additionally, when coaching online, the use of a curated digital library of images means the same doors are frequently used.
11 In Greek mythology Psyche (meaning breath of life i.e., soul or spirit) was represented by a butterfly.

Bibliography

Carlson, K., Flanagin, M., Martin, K., Martin, M., Mendelsohn, J., Young Rodgers, P., Ronnberg, A., Salman, S., & Wesley, D. (2010). *The Book of Symbols*. Taschen.

Crick, R. D., & Grushka, K. (2009). Signs, symbols and metaphor: linking self with text in inquiry-based learning. *The Curriculum Journal, 20*(4), 447–464. https://doi.org/10.1080/0958517090 3425069

de Botton, A., & Armstrong, J. (2013). *Art as Therapy*. Phaidon.

Foglia, L., & Wilson, R. (2017). *Embodied Cognition, The Stanford Encyclopedia of Philosophy*. https://plato.stanford.edu/archives/spr2017/entries/embodied-cognition/.

Foglia, L., & Wilson, R. A. (2013). Embodied cognition. *Wiley Interdisciplinary Reviews: Cognitive Science, 4*(3), 319–325. https://doi.org/10.1002/wcs.1226

Jung, C. G., Henderson, J. L., Jacobi, J., Jaffé, A., & Franz, M.-L. vo. (1964). *Man and his Symbols* (C. G. Jung & M.-L. vo. Franz (eds.)). Aldus Books Ltd.

Lakoff, G. (2012). Explaining Embodied Cognition Results. *Topics in Cognitive Science, 4*(4), 773–785. https://doi.org/10.1111/j.1756-8765.2012.01222.x

Lakoff, G., & Johnson, M. (1980). *Metaphors We Live By*. The University of Chicago Press.

9   Creativity in Coaching

PART 1 | A COMPELLING CASE FOR CREATIVITY IN COACHING

Creativity in Coaching

The International Coaching Federation (2020) defines coaching as "Partnering with clients in a thought-provoking and **creative process**[1] that inspires them to maximise their personal and professional potential." Creativity is therefore recognised as a valuable and contributing factor to successful coaching.

Once thought to be a gift, or personality trait, belonging to a select group of exceptional individuals (often described as creative geniuses), creativity still retains an air of mystique. Fortunately, extensive research and literature on the topic confirm that everyone possesses the capacity for creative expression. Therefore, it is possible to identify, nurture, and develop it as a skill.

Defining Creativity

"Creativity is characterised by the ability to perceive the world in new ways. To find hidden patterns, to make connections between seemingly unrelated phenomena, and to generate solutions." (Anonymous) This definition aligns well with the Collage Coaching Technique™ (CCT).

The earliest definitions emphasised the requirement for novelty or originality, as well as usefulness in the product. Not to say that creativity in coaching does not fit that description, because when referring to art-making in coaching Falato (2012. para. 4) states, "The act of spontaneously generating something that has not been there before … demands the presence of original vision." Furthermore, clients experience new insights and a-ha moments that are important novel thoughts for enabling breakthroughs. Additionally, as a useful end product, the collage performs a pivotal role in personal development. However, for clients, the focus is not solely on eliciting original thoughts. They are also interested in seeking and achieving clarity, focus, awareness, and progress. Therefore, shifting focus unto the process significantly reframes clients' expectations and creative experience.

There are numerous models aimed at qualifying the creative process.[2] The following two are amongst those that reflect the theory and approach found in the CCT. Guilford's 4 stage model of divergent thinking and Beghetto and J. C. Kaufman's Four C Model of creativity.

DOI: 10.4324/9781003017028-11

Guilford described creativity as four distinct sequential steps: preparation, incubation, illumination, and verification (Lubart, 2001). Although he recognised this did not occur without other influences, this model served as the framework from which many others emerged. Subsequent research argues that there are additional steps and that the process is not sequential but moves back and forth between them according to the problem at hand. Despite these differences, researchers in this field primarily agree that the creative process moves through several stages.

The Four C model distinguishes levels of creativity, not intending to test innate ability but to identify the degree to which an individual expresses their own (Helfand et al., 2016). While acknowledging that all are valid and valuable, this model suggests an increasing level of endeavour and output moves an individual through Mini, Little, Pro, and Big-C creativity. Clients are likely to predominantly enter coaching with experience of Mini-C, which concerns everyday, less prominent creative acts. Examples include experimenting with recipes, different combinations of attire, or finding more efficient ways to organise a study. Beghetto & J. C. Kaufman (2007) stress the value of Mini-C as an act of internal development through introspection, with a focus on the process rather than output, therefore removing the need for external judgement or acceptance. In this creative space, individuals deliberately encounter new information and experiences that enable them to grow and make progress that has significant personal meaning. However, in western cultures, at least, Mini-C contributions are often overlooked and dismissed, including by the client who does not always understand these activities as a form of creative expression. Furthermore, society tends to focus attention on Big-C contributors and their accomplishments. These are individuals who transform the domain in which they work, for instance, Bob Marley, Georgia O'keefe, or Albert Einstein.

To redress this imbalance and provide a broader perspective, it is worth sharing an overview of Beghetto and J. C. Kaufman's model with clients. This information is especially relevant where an individual's perception is adversely impacting them from engaging with their creativity. For these clients, knowledge of the Four C Model could help them embrace their capacity for meaningful creative acts and add immense value to their lives and others.

Case Study | Revealing Creativity in the Workplace

Andrew is a maths teacher who was frustrated with his job and considering leaving his profession. He struggled when delivering his lessons, feeling constrained by the externally imposed rules and guidelines that he described as onerous. While acknowledging they existed due to the syllabus and examinations, it didn't change his view that the majority were bureaucratic, unnecessary and time-consuming. Andrew also saw these practices as limiting opportunities to be more creative and engaging in his work with students. As he used the image to discuss these feelings, Andrew spoke of a man who enjoyed being creative and messy, describing the photograph as aspirational. In response to the question, "Is there anything else about the image?" Andrew noticed that the background colours mirrored the ones on the man. The only difference was that the former appeared as distinct shapes and outlines, including a triangle, which he described as ironically mathematical. Andrew continued exploring the connection between the colours on the man and the background. He came to see himself as the former, while teaching (his ideal view of it) was the latter. In this instance, the colours meant they matched perfectly, reflecting his desire for his career. Through ongoing discussion, he shared some of his teaching

Figure 9.1.1 Photograph by Pavan K Gireesh on Unsplash.

methods, including using one resource in multiple ways, deliberately seeking to create richer learning experiences and ensuring teaching materials met different students' needs. At this point, I shared the Four C Model of creativity and elicited his thoughts around his lesson planning from this perspective. He replied that he had not considered maths teaching as having any connection to creativity until now. However, equipped with his image and a new creative perspective, Andrew professed feeling more energised, willing, and confident concerning his potential for developing his creative output in his current role, despite external constraints.

Benefits of Creativity for Clients

In coaching, creativity greatly assists self-development because it is an opportunity for individual, independent, and lateral thinking that stimulates personal problem-solving.[3] The value in enabling this creative thought process via an arts-based method (ABM) is threefold.

Firstly, with a focus on exploration and discovery, the process includes the following immediate benefits for clients:

- exposure to new ways of looking, seeing, and consequently thinking
- unlocking knowledge that leads to insights and deeper self-awareness
- enabling new internal and external experiences
- engendering a sense of pride and achievement in creating something tangible

"I didn't think I'd be able to do it as I'm not a creative person, but I'm so pleased with my collage. I think I'll frame it." (Claire)

Longer-term, and with repeated application of ABMs, skills transfer can expand clients' development in the following ways:

- learning to accept and work with uncertainty and ambiguity
- increased confidence in their problem-solving skills through recognising the possibility of multiple solutions
- reducing aversion to risk-taking
- integration of seemingly opposite ways of thinking
- understanding when it is time to let go of certain beliefs or behaviours

Secondly, understanding the creative process through participation in an ABM allows clients to recognise its attributes and how it exhibits in their daily experiences. This knowledge can help a client begin to nurture and develop a personal brand of creative expression. Consequently, empowering them to harness, release, increase, and apply this creative energy to pursue their goals and intentions, potentially leading them to progress from Mini to Little-C.[4] With the latter, individuals feel confident developing their creative ideas and sharing them publicly (Beghetto & J. C. Kaufman, 2007). However, until clients are aware of and accept their innate creative ability, they cannot apply it in a deliberate and focused manner to support development in different areas of their lives. Furthermore, as a form of energy, creativity does not lie dormant when not utilised. Instead, it is redirected into other processes and potentially less favourable modes of self-expression, such as fear, frustration, judgement, and resentment (Goldenberg et al., 1999).

Lastly, creativity is an essential skill in an increasingly VUCA (volatile, uncertain, complex, and ambiguous) world. As an invaluable tool for problem-solving, ongoing and intentional use increases a client's agility and flexibility to respond to rapid personal or professional change. Accordingly, the onus of coaching with collage is on the process, because as Taylor & Ladkin (2009) maintain, this ensures knowledge and skills acquired concerning creativity are transferable. This focus is consistent with the Eastern philosophy of creativity, which emphasises personal development rather than the Western view that predominantly concerns the output.

Myths and Misconceptions | Blocks to Creative Expression

The purpose of exploring and explaining the nature of creativity from a scientific, evidence-based perspective recognises that:

1   Individuals who do not consider themselves artistically creative can understand how it manifests in all areas of life.
2   Some clients and coaches are interested in, prefer, and benefit from learning about the process first, rather than experientially.

1. Creativity Equals Art

Creativity does not equal art.

At its core, creativity involves a mental process and adopting an attitude of childlike curiosity that suspends preconceived judgements, takes risks, and remains open to new ideas. Creativity, therefore, does not necessarily lead to the production of a tangible output. When it does develop in this way, for example, in art, dance, poetry, film, music, design technology, or other disciplines, it still involves the internal neurological process and the childlike approach.

Unsurprisingly, many people do not understand the cognitive process behind creativity because the overriding perception is that it equals art. Therefore, without the skills or training to reach a preconceived standard of artistic output, they fail to recognise it in themselves. Additionally, people who say they are not creative express this not with enthusiasm but with a sense of resignation and regret.

In coaching, this flawed perception can cause anxiety for both clients and coaches, acting as a block to engagement with ABMs. This apprehension may be rooted in experiences at school where art is usually evaluated through grading rather than encouraged as a form of personal visual expression. In drawing comparisons, notions of what constitutes right or wrong and good or bad art become accepted as the norm. Consequently, for many students, robbing them of the creative confidence and freedom they formerly enjoyed, that then continues into adulthood. Most often expressed as, "I can't draw," or "I'm no good at art." In his famous Ted Talk, "Do schools kill creativity?" Sir Ken Robinson (2006) alludes to this when he says, "We get educated out of creativity." Anecdotal evidence from numerous clients, all with similar stories about their negative art experience at school, supports his theory. While many coaches aspire to add a creative approach to their practice, invariably, they acknowledge a lack of confidence to pursue this goal, with the root cause usually the same as for clients. In response to this, the 'Collage as a Creative Coaching Tool' training programme was developed.

The following statements serve to alleviate these types of concerns:

* This approach is not about your perceived level of artistic or creative skills.
* You cannot do it wrong.
* Do not judge yourself or others (the latter relates to group work); I certainly will not be judging you.

Setting this foundation is essential because the language[5] used when introducing and guiding clients through the creative process is vital for empowering their engagement when using an ABM in coaching. Additionally, adding humour when referring to art experiences at school is another strategy that recognises, validates, and then seeks to reduce negative associations.

2. Creativity Is a Right-Brain Activity

Creativity is a whole-brain approach.

Another common misconception concerning creativity is the divide between the brain's left and right hemispheres. The hypothesis is that individuals think and function predominantly from either side, with the right dominant for those who are more artistic, intuitive, and creative, while the left pre-disposes individuals to a more language centric, analytical, and logical way of thinking. Unfortunately, this concept is reinforced by images depicting the right hemisphere as colourful and decorative. In stark contrast, the left is usually grey or black and linear. By representing them using deliberately juxtaposing shapes and colours, emphasis is placed on the hemispheres as opposites, visually perpetuating the belief that "never the twain shall meet." Therefore, this imagery incorrectly says the side of the brain an individual is predisposed to use fundamentally predetermines their creative ability.

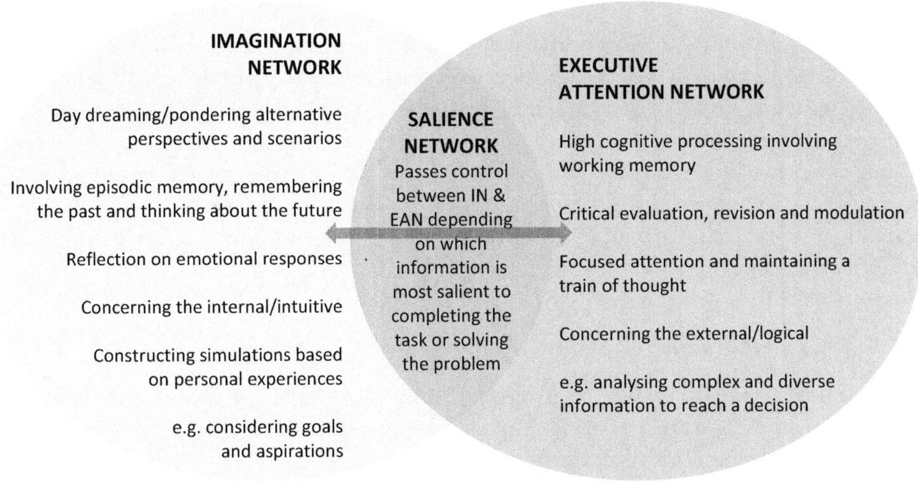

IMAGINATION NETWORK

Day dreaming/pondering alternative perspectives and scenarios

Involving episodic memory, remembering the past and thinking about the future

Reflection on emotional responses

Concerning the internal/intuitive

Constructing simulations based on personal experiences

e.g. considering goals and aspirations

SALIENCE NETWORK

Passes control between IN & EAN depending on which information is most salient to completing the task or solving the problem

EXECUTIVE ATTENTION NETWORK

High cognitive processing involving working memory

Critical evaluation, revision and modulation

Focused attention and maintaining a train of thought

Concerning the external/logical

e.g. analysing complex and diverse information to reach a decision

Figure 9.1.2 The Neuroscience of Creativity.
Source: The Real Neuroscience of Creativity (S. B. Kaufman, 2013).
Creative Cognition and Brain Network Dynamics (Beaty et al., 2016).

Although certain processes occur in specific brain regions (for example, processing language takes place in the Broca's and Wernicke's areas located in the left hemisphere), MRI scans reveal a continuous relaying of information between the hemispheres (Turney, 2018). Creativity is no different, and ongoing research in this area shows a cognitive process involving two large brain networks, the Imagination and Executive Attention, located across both hemispheres. A third, the Salience network, is responsible for passing information between the other networks, with the former expanding thinking and the latter contracting it to evaluate and draw conclusions. Figure 9.2 illustrates the relationship and roles of these networks.

The Neuroscience of Creativity

The Imagination Network

The Imagination (IN) or Default network was first identified by the neurologist Marcus Raichle in 2001. As the domain of divergent thinking, activity in this region is highest when the mind is left to roam, for instance, when daydreaming or pondering. Researchers' term this activity self-generated thoughts or cognition, and it occurs regardless of whether there is an end goal to the ruminations. The IN is responsible for mental simulation, autobiographical retrieval, perspective-taking, and episodic future thinking (S. B. Kaufman, 2013; Beaty et al., 2016).

Together these functions enable imagining the future and remembering the past, which is necessary for making meaning of personal experiences that then inform and direct future goals. The IN also encompasses the medial regions of the temporal lobe, which enable reflection on emotional responses and engenders feelings of compassion.[6]

The Executive Attention Network

The Executive Attention Network (EAN) controls working memory and is responsible for monitoring external events and focusing imagination and attention (S. B. Kaufman, 2013; Beaty et al., 2016). Consequently, it is activated when there is a need to employ high cognitive processes. For instance, when problem-solving and reasoning, or analysing complex and diverse information to reach a decision. During the creative process, because the EAN focuses attention, it is thought to monitor and control goal-directed behaviours[7] by maintaining a train of thought and disregarding information that is not pertinent to a successful outcome.

The Salience Network and Coupling

With the IN primarily related to internal stimuli and the EAN to external ones, they appear as directly opposing networks, equivalent to the portrayal of the left and right brain hemispheres. At times, this distinction does apply, resulting in a conflict where logic may override intuition or vice versa. However, during the creative process, research proves they work co-operatively through the Salience Network, in what is known as coupling (Beaty et al., 2016). The salience network monitors both internal (IN) and external (EAN) consciousness, transmitting pertinent information back and forth between the two until identifying a suitable solution to solve the task at hand.

Overall, the studies conclude that while the IN allows for divergent and bottom-up thinking, the EAN is responsible for top-down critical evaluation. The latter involves revision and moderation of the ideas, emotions, and information retrieved through the IN before deciding which will best serve the present goal. Within this exchange, both emotional and cognitive, spontaneous and intentional thought processes are involved in decision making.

Coaching Creatively with Collage

"The key to understanding the neuroscience of creativity lies not only in knowledge of these large scale networks, but in recognising that different patterns of neural activations and deactivations are important at different stages of the creative process", asserts (S. B. Kaufman, 2013, para. 12). This assertion is undoubtedly the case regarding the CCT. Following Guilford's model of divergent thinking, the emphasis is on opening thinking and leaving selection and evaluation until later. Therefore, the IN is activated first as clients intuitively gather a collection of images, enabling them to engage in lateral thinking, access their unconscious, expand possibilities, and silence their inner critic. As an activity designed to reduce activation of the EAN, the guidance for clients is to disregard intrusive analytical thoughts.

Each stage flows into the following with a natural break that differentiates the neural processes. When clients transition into creating their collage, partial activation of the EAN is encouraged by directing them to become consciously aware of their internal dialogue. The purpose for clients in focusing some attention here is to become aware of the analysis, reflection, and mental modification occurring through meaning-making while creating their collage. During this entire process, both external and internal, unconscious and conscious, emotional and analytical thinking flow back and forth, as the salience network regularly switches the creative process between the IN and EAN.

In line with models of the creative process, as clients commence the final stage of the CCT, the IN recedes, as it is time for their EAN to function as the dominant network. Enabled by the storytelling and coaching conversation, this activation involves clients sharing and exploring the symbolic images, visual metaphors, and other aspects of their collage story with their coach. As an outward form of creative and immensely personal self-expression, it becomes a valuable resource for the EAN to work with as it evaluates, verifies, consolidates, and integrates relevant information. Consequently, as new mental and emotional models begin to take shape, the insights, breakthroughs, decisions, and other information learnt through the process are now available for clients to use in a purposeful way towards their desired outcomes.

In summary, the CCT can be understood as a metaphor for the creative process because each stage plays a specific role in flexibly activating or partially deactivating the brain networks involved in creativity. Firstly, allowing an opening of ideas, thoughts, and feelings followed by evaluation and verification. As an arts-based coaching tool, it benefits from combining both experiential and cognitive creative processes, which naturally results in coupling the IN and EAN. Enhancement of this joining occurs due to the use of images, which, as the source of clients' knowledge and insights, hold both unconscious (internal) and conscious (external) information.[8] Therefore, even during the cognitive querying and evaluation, clients are never entirely divorced from their intuitive or emotional knowledge, which is available for immediate reference through the image as source material.

Client Reflections | Curiosity Did Not Kill the Cat

The following narrative is a personal account by Nicholas, someone who saw himself as naturally analytical. As he shares his experience, Nicholas describes how coaching with collage helped develop his creative confidence. Particularly in enabling him to access and work with information from the unconscious in tandem with his more familiar cognitive approaches.

"I saw the collage as using a tool, producing something I could gain insight from, which enabled me to uncover a story. There was something about consciously uncovering what was unconsciously known, but never articulated, and saying 'Actually, do you know what? this is what happens and it's okay.' I usually have a very analytical, precise and process-driven approach, and alongside that I took advantage of the unlocking, surfacing, and working beyond conscious thinking, so was able to use both my analytical and

Figure 9.1.3 Nicholas' collage.

unconscious knowledge. The fact that it generates critical thought and reflection, that is insightful and useful is the important thing.

One of the valuable insights I gained was appreciation of the cycles I go through, and that's about relationships and roles, experiences as well as project work, and how I genuinely feel at different points in time. Recognising those three phases from the metaphor for curiosity with the kitten, through to the challenges and the loneliness of the discovery and the journey of the strident tiger, to the proud accomplished lion, but that also includes the judgment aspect of being watched. That was really useful and important, and I know those came out as a result of the conversations that I wouldn't have had if I hadn't done the collage.

Even though I wasn't looking at the collage regularly, I do revisit it and over time it's made things easier. Firstly, being more assured and effective on projects by reducing the sense of panic at particular stages (it's like knowing you're about to go on the scary part of the rollercoaster but it will come back to rest). It's allowed me to become a more confident me, more reassured irrespective of the complexity and messiness of where we are. Not to say I go through life in a meditative state, but around certain things, particularly projects or new challenges or experiences, I'm able to take a more realistic perspective. I think in moments of high stress and complexity things can feel quite threatening and that can start a downward spiral. So that's been a little bit easier because I know the upward (or even level) trajectory always follows the downward spiral. Secondly, it's also helped me reflect on the need to take time out, especially in Tiger phase. Because there is a point where projects are a bit more complicated and with the pride of lions you don't have to be alone through the different phases. I've realised I just need different people, and forms of support at different points.

Although I didn't have a distinct goal or plan when I created my collage, it encouraged me and gave me confidence to be open to other opportunities that I might have shut myself off from. That is also reflected in some of the work that I've done since, because it's been easier to hold the messier outcomes when trying to lead and coach change in organisations, to challenge and hold accountability at the highest levels.

In terms of my creative aspects, it's given me greater permission to explore messier ways forwards to achieve things. Even in my relationship with LEGO® it's stopped me taking such a technical approach, it inspired me to just play more in terms of trying to produce things and just seeing what happens, like I did when I was younger, building vignettes of bits of pieces rather than just sets to instructions.

While I think my creativity has always been there, because of my analytical and project management roles, which are often technical, I probably became a bit more guarded in my thinking and writing, and it's definitely relaxed that. So, permission, confidence to experiment and comfort with messiness were key benefits from doing it." (Dr Nicholas)

Dr Nicholas' reflections illustrate how engaging with the creative process in coaching can assist clients in their professional and personal life. Experiencing an increase in creative confidence, transference of knowledge to other domains, and accepting the more uncomfortable, messy aspects of life is an outcome applicable to all clients coached with the CCT.

3. Creativity Is Messy and Chaotic

Creativity works within constraints.

Because of its strong association with 'the arts,' creativity is often considered a messy and chaotic activity that encourages unbridled self-expression with no apparent restraint or focus. Stereotyped images associated with creativity (frequently depicted as multiple bright, mixed colours, paint marks, and splashes) reinforce this impression, while the 'creative' person is invariably attired unconventionally.

While the outcomes of a creative process are not entirely predictable, this is not the same as chaotic. In fact, within 'the arts' sector, artists work within what is known as 'creative constraints.' For example, in jazz music, improv, and the visual arts, each discipline, or individual artist, works with self-imposed rules and guidelines designed to create order within creativity and keep things moving forward. In jazz, it might be restricting the use of a major scale, defining the pitch or loudness of notes for the ensemble. For improv, there are rules such as 'yes–and,' 'make statements,' and 'focus on the here and now.' While in the visual arts, contrary to how they may appear, artists such as Jackson Pollock create paintings within clearly defined limits concerning colour choice and how paint is applied.

These constraints exist, because in the absence of clear direction or a guiding framework, there is a risk of disarray and failure to deliver anything of actual value or purpose (Goldenberg et al., 1999; S. B. Kaufman, 2013). Participants in such a creative process are likely to experience a combination of anxiety, confusion, frustration, and potentially anger. Therefore, when introducing a creative approach in coaching, although it may sound restrictive, undesirable, and counter-productive, constraints are necessary to provide the parameters in which individuals or groups can find meaningful expression. In group work, these are imperative if members are to succeed at reaching a consensus.

As with all schools of thought, there is an opposing argument. In this instance, the contrary view is that boundaries limit creative output (Amabile, 2006, as cited by Onarheim & Wiltschnig, 2010). However, most of the research undertaken in psychology, design, and organisations on this topic, surmise that results are better when there is a balance between them. At the same time recognising that the form and duration of constraints will influence how people perceive and respond to specific limitations. Furthermore, many writers in the field assert that introducing creative constraints ensures the activity can be evaluated and enhances the creative results (Caniëls & Rietzschel, 2015; Goldenberg et al., 1999; Onarheim & Wiltschnig, 2010). Evidence suggests reasons for this include the most pertinent information surfacing and participants adapting and being resourceful.

In the design domain, Onarheim & Wiltschnig (2010) also argue that because everyone has to operate within constructs, implementing boundaries means creative skills are more likely to be transferable. These constructs may manifest as financial, psychological, personal, and professional limitations for coaching clients, including organisational procedures and requirements. Therefore, developing individual creativity within parameters ensures clients anticipate constraints as they apply their new skills outside of the coaching environment. Furthermore, they are better able to recognise whether these limitations facilitate or hinder the creative process.

Coaching with Constraints

In the CCT, constraints within the creative process include:

- an agreed theme
- three defined stages
- specific guidance for each stage
- set lengths of time per stage

Whether external (as part of the process) or internal (as the neurological function of the EAN), incorporating defined limits is designed to empower rather than curtail an individual's creativity. Therefore, before the consultation, clients are informed of these constraints and their purpose in providing focus while reducing complexity, cognitive override, and creative inhibitions. Crucially, knowing there is clear guidance and a sequential structure to follow manages expectations, builds trust, and alleviates anxiety concerning the unfamiliar. As indicated by feedback such as, "I'm glad it was time-limited, if I'd had longer to create the collage, I know I would have started overthinking and doubting myself," and "It really helped knowing what the next stage was. It meant I could be in the moment, without worrying what you would ask us to do next."

Simultaneously, this framework is a container, that safe space where clients can create without inhibitions or fear of failure,[9] which is unequivocally central to enabling personal development through creative expression. As these sets of constraints remove focus away from the question, "Am I doing this right?" creative energy is released to flow elsewhere. Metaphorically, this physical and psychological creative space can be visualised as a children's playground with benches for parents or guardians, enclosed by a fence. The child knows that within the fence, they have the freedom to explore and play without limitations. Sometimes the equipment is unavailable or off-limits, but the child can play with what is available, adapt and be resourceful. In which case, the only limitation is the extent of their imagination. It is the same for clients. Within the safety of creative constraints, knowing the coach is available if necessary, they have complete freedom for curiosity, self-expression, personal insights, and discovery.

Awareness of this structural approach is particularly beneficial for clients who appreciate defined parameters. Examples include leaders and organisations who prefer working within frameworks, individuals who consider themselves left-brained, or those with less creative confidence. Therefore, clarifying the CCT as a three-stage process, using language clients recognise, such as framework, parameters, structure, or requirements, helps lay a foundation for successful engagement with creative coaching techniques.

Overall, as a creative tool for exploration and discovery, problem-solving and change, coaching with collage yields better results when its focus and energy remain within boundaries. For those not used to arts-based approaches, the alternative can feel like being handed a blank sheet of paper and asked to draw anything!

4. Creativity and Destruction

Akin to the word constraints, destruction generally holds negative connotations. However, it plays an integral role in creativity because, in the process of creating something new, another thing is destroyed. In this context, destruction is not about annihilation, devastation, or ruin. Instead, it refers to disintegration and loss of form or structure as something transforms. During the CCT, it is clear what is initially destroyed and re-formed. Magazines, as familiar everyday objects designed for reading, are cut and torn, rendering them no longer fit for their original purpose. Yet, through the gathered images, clients draw together fragments of their memories, thoughts, ideas, influences, values, emotions, and hopes for the future to create something new.

On occasion, clients find it difficult to destroy the magazines in this way. Sometimes they struggle to make the mental shift from magazines as reading material to seeing them as an arts-based medium. Other times, it is concern about wasting the images they may not use, causing reluctance to remove all that resonates with them. In these scenarios, clients are reassured and reminded that the magazines are a resource provided expressly for use in this fashion. As they make a conscious shift in how they perceive the magazines, for the duration of the creative process, it is another form of defamiliarising the familiar[5] that promotes movement away from habitual ways of seeing and thinking. Reimagining how they relate to the magazines holds potential as a transferrable skill to view situations from an alternative perspective and expand perceptions.

In terms of dismantling the original structure of the magazines, this destruction is also a symbolic representation of the clients' internal thoughts. Initially, they gather images from magazines as an accessible and familiar product. In the same way, and simultaneously, they also first work with and explore their existing patterns of behaviours, emotions, and mindsets. Once taken out of context, the images are deconstructed, reshaped, reassembled, and combined with other sources to take on a new form and alternative meaning. As the creator, the client, like an artist, has complete control over this transformational process of destroying and recreating.

Both like, and through this process of manipulating their images, clients' current emotions, habits, assumptions, behaviours, and mindsets are either diminished, destroyed, re-formed, or affirmed as aspects of the self are preserved, let go, or changed.[10] This transformation is an exchange akin to a caterpillar's metamorphosis into a butterfly. During the CCT, this change may occur instantaneously or over more extended periods.[11]

Awareness of the duality between the destructive and creative nature of working with the CCT supports the client's development. For instance, as a holistic approach, there is value in reflecting on experiences of loss alongside personal gains. One way to facilitate this is by guiding clients to notice the images they discard when deciding which ones to use in their collage. Recognition of what may be lost includes awareness of mindsets, attitudes, and behaviours that are not serving them well. However, it could also relate to letting go of longstanding relationships and careers, which may prove a more difficult task. Fortunately, like an artist, clients can learn to become more comfortable with renewal through loss as an outcome of the creative process. Examples include when clients become aware they possess the creative efficacy to reshape their future following redundancy or divorce.

Capitalising on Creativity

Arguably, as 'the arts' naturally facilitate the creative process, an effective way to promote and develop creative problem-solving skills is through practicing these approaches. However, it should be remembered that commonly held ideas of good and bad art, the perception of it being messy, and the myths concerning the characteristics of a creative person means engaging in personal creative expression takes courage on the client's part.

In deconstructing the creative process, the purpose of this chapter is to address these misconceptions and provide information and insight necessary to help demystify clients' and coaches' understanding of creative expression. Nonetheless, sight is never lost of coaching with collage as a creative force that engenders inspiration, joy, release, and accomplishment for many clients. As these are frequent occurrences, witnessing clients' satisfaction, pleasure, and pride in their collage as an output of their coaching session is something coaches can look forward to experiencing. Furthermore, the CCT promotes understanding and appreciation of all forms of creativity, as prescribed in the Four C model. Accordingly, regardless of the broader impact, clients have an opportunity to identify and harness their personal brand. Occasionally, this occurs through creating their collage, as they discover a latent talent for the visual arts. For all involved, these are exciting moments to experience and enjoy.

As a transferable skill, knowledge of the attributes of creativity informs clients and coaches regarding the actions or attention necessary at different stages of the process. Whether in the coaching context or beyond, this proves valuable concerning awareness of when to enable the opening of divergent thinking, focus attention on evaluation, or implement creative constraints. Appreciation of the duality of the CCT as a process that combines creativity and destruction is another lesson clients are encouraged to embrace. Because in acknowledging this concept, they can learn to accept there is always an element of loss alongside renewal and that the power to recreate is in their hands, as embodied when they created their collage. Ultimately, this recognition can make transitions more manageable as clients redirect their creative energy to their goals and intentions.

Bibliography

Beaty, R. E., Benedek, M., Silvia, P. J., & Schacter, D. L. (2016). Creative Cognition and Brain Network Dynamics. In *Trends in Cognitive Sciences*, 20(1), 87–95). Elsevier Ltd. https://doi.org/10.1016/j.tics.2015.10.004

Beghetto, R. A., & Kaufman, J. C. (2007). Toward a broader conception of creativity: A case for "mini-c" creativity. *Psychology of Aesthetics, Creativity, and the Arts*, 1(2), 73–79. https://doi.org/10.1037/1931-3896.1.2.73

Caniëls, M. C. J., & Rietzschel, E. F. (2015). Organizing creativity: Creativity and innovation under constraints. *Creativity and Innovation Management*, 24(2), 184–196. https://doi.org/10.1111/caim.12123

Falato, D. (2012). *How Using Art Making as a Coaching Tool Supports Client Learning*. International Coach Academy. https://coachcampus.com/coach-portfolios/research-papers/dawn-falato-how-using-art-making-as-a-coaching-tool-supports-client-learning/

Goldenberg, J., Mazursky, D., & Solomon, S. (1999). Creative sparks. In *Science* (Vol. 285, Issue 5433, pp. 1495–1496). American Association for the Advancement of Science. https://doi.org/10.1126/science.285.5433.1495

Helfand, M., Kaufman, J. C., & Beghetto, R. A. (2016). The Four-C Model of Creativity: Culture and Context. In *The Palgrave Handbook of Creativity and Culture Research* (pp. 15–36). Palgrave Macmillan UK. https://doi.org/10.1057/978-1-137-46344-9_2

International Coaching Federation. (2020). https://coachfederation.org/about

Kaufman, S. B. (2013). *The Real Neuroscience of Creativity - Scientific American Blog Network*. Beautiful Minds. https://blogs.scientificamerican.com/beautiful-minds/the-real-neuroscience-of-creativity/

Lubart, T. I. (2001). Models of the creative process: Past, present and future. *Creativity Research Journal*, 13(3–4), 295–308. https://doi.org/10.1207/s15326934crj1334_07

Onarheim, B., & Wiltschnig, S. (2010). *Opening and Constraining: Constraints and Their Role in Creative Processes*.

Robinson, K. (2006). *Do schools kill creativity? | TED Talk*. www.ted.com/talks/sir_ken_robinson_do_schools_kill_creativity?language=en

Taylor, S. S., & Ladkin, D. (2009). Understanding arts-based methods in managerial development. *Academy of Management Learning and Education*, 8(1), 55–69. https://doi.org/10.5465/AMLE.2009.37012179

Turney, J. (2018). *Cracking Neuroscience*. Octopus Publishing Group.

PART 2 | THE CREATIVE PROCESS AS AN EXPRESSION OF 'SELF'

Some of the content in this chapter section refers primarily to creating the classic version of a coaching collage, which uses magazines rather than the online digital version.[12]

Projective Techniques

The use of projective techniques began in the field of psychoanalysis, pioneered mainly by Sigmund Freud. The method involves using a range of stimuli, including words, visuals, and objects to access unconscious and hidden content, emotions, and whatever may be difficult to articulate (Porr et al., 2011). Their purpose is to offer clients a way to bypass potential barriers of cognition, automatic responses, and rational thought that diffuse or suppress honest expression. Therefore, projective techniques allow uncensored ideas, judgements, feelings, and other material to find a voice through external objects, images, and associative words (Branthwaite, 2002). Consequently, potentially challenging yet valuable information becomes available to the individual.

Based on this explanation, by default, the Collage Coaching Technique™(CCT) is a projective technique. According to Porr et al. (2011), there are four types of projection, of which the CCT would be defined as constructive. Using visual metaphors and symbols to access the unconscious intensifies a coaching collage's projective qualities. This enhanced outcome results because a client's projected 'self,' or circumstances existing in the externalised objects, are also understood in terms of something else, creating layers of meaning for exploration.[13]

When coaching groups, the projection inherent in the CCT enables discussion of different perspectives to focus on the image, rather than as views held by individuals.[14] This approach creates a more conducive environment for the collective exploration of issues affecting the group and its members, such as organisational culture (Colakoglu & Littlefield, 2011). Other methodologies that employ projective techniques include LEGO®Serious Play® (LSP) and the Zaltman Metaphorical Elicitation Technique (ZMET®).

The Stories We Tell Ourselves

In the coaching profession, the significance of 'the stories we tell ourselves' is well understood. Whether referring to those that help clients build confidence and thrive or create blocks and diminish their potential, these stories also exist as images in the mind.

Branthwaite (2002) describes how imagined objects and ideas projected outwards have almost the same effects on the unconscious mind as if they were real.[15] Visualisation works on this basis and is recommended as a technique to help clients achieve their goals. Rather than focusing on avoiding failure, they create a mental image of a pre-determined goal and the necessary actions for success. Constant repetition of these projections entrenches the initial thought and increases its perception as something already achieved (Martin & Schwartz, 2014). Consequently, acting in accordance with this belief, the client moves towards their goal with a confident attitude. However, unless an individual is intentional, the mind does not discern which images to visualise. Therefore, it can also project internalised detrimental beliefs around identity, experiences, abilities, self-worth, and so forth that are unhelpful to positive self-development.

Nevertheless, inside every person is their authentic self, albeit masked by perpetual negative self-talk, false ideas, and conditioned behaviour. To enable change and experience this version of themselves, clients must first become aware of their internal stories and associated imagery. Only in having a complete understanding of this can they reconnect with, believe and trust in who they are to release the power of their original story (Fitzpatrick, 2014). The CCT facilitates this awareness by drawing these images and stories, both false and authentic, from the internal unconscious to the external conscious mind.

Connecting with the Unconscious

While it may seem like an oxymoron, to connect to the unconscious mind requires conscious action. Otherwise, clients are likely to find it difficult to let go of the rationalising and editing process that results from cognition wanting to comprehend why images resonate. Facilitating the process of engaging with the unconscious includes clear guidance and potentially a mindfulness exercise,[16] both ensure the mind focuses on the present and is aware of distracting thoughts. However, because cognitive processing is the default position, the coach should understand that there will always be clients who find it challenging to follow the principal instruction, "Take every image that resonates with you." In recognition of this challenge, besides the initial guidance, the coach remains mindfully observant of clients, watching as they look through and noticing if they are filtering their choices.

A clear example of this is when they look at an image for an extended period, as though they are examining it, but then turn the page. At times, the client may flick a page backwards and forwards, considering what they are looking at and still leave it behind. This behaviour is usually indicative of conscious decision making rather than following intuitive guidance. The more clients remain with cognitive reasoning, the longer it takes them to access their unconscious. To negate this approach, the coach periodically reminds them to take every image without question and repeats other core guidance.

Transferable Knowledge

Every stage of the CCT provides sources of learning and insight for clients. Consequently, while gathering, there are opportunities for self-development and awareness-raising if the client, supported by the coach, is willing to explore what materialises as they engage with the magazines.

An example of this is noticing assumptions and judgements conveyed when clients describe *The Economist* as boring, gardening magazines as weird, *The Rugby Magazine* being for men while *Cloth-Paper-Scissors* is for women. These definitions influence clients' perceptions and willingness to use certain titles. To prevent their judgements from acting as an obstacle to engaging with the unconscious mind, they are guided to take magazines as they come rather than filter through the pile. This guidance prevents clients' preconceived ideas of what they expect to find in their preferred magazines, compared to those they would normally reject, having a detrimental impact on their outcomes.

In working without assumptions, clients frequently come across an image that perfectly captures what they need to express, moves them towards their goal or resolves inner conflict. When originating from a magazine they would have dismissed, they acquire a valuable lesson in adopting a more open mindset. This knowledge is transferable and available for use beyond the coaching environment. Equally, the coach does not allow personal judgements to affect client experiences by censoring the available magazine choice.

The following case studies are other examples of clients' transferable learning experiences during the gathering stage.

Case Study | Slowing Down

Clients reflect on their coaching session by answering the question, "And what do you know now?" After one session, a client replied, "I've learnt the importance of slowing down." She arrived at this conclusion after being asked to do this while looking through the magazines. I had noticed she was turning pages too fast to connect with any of the images. She shared how decreasing her pace had caused images to start resonating with her, unlike before. As a result, she saw a correlation between reduced speed during the activity and slowing down in other areas of her life to lower stress and be more appreciative of the present moment.

Case Study | Relinquishing the Need to Control

During a small group session, Alex chose not to follow the instructions and instead selected specific magazines. When the time came to create her collage, she mentioned not finding enough images in the magazines because some were missing that she may have wanted. (Being reused, these gaps appear where clients have already removed pictures and words. Nevertheless, enough remain to make the magazine a viable resource.) Alex also believed the choice was not broad enough. When asked what led her to that conclusion, she replied, "I couldn't find the images I wanted." This response indicated she had remained with cognitive thinking and decision making rather than being guided by her intuitive unconscious. Because she was intentional about her image choice, Alex probably overlooked images that would have resonated with her in the magazines she chose, as well as those she dismissed.

I reminded her of the initial guidance and how working with the unconscious meant letting go of preconceived ideas, including magazine and image choice. Alex responded by sharing her recognition that she had wanted to remain in control of the process, finding it difficult to allow things to emerge. Furthermore, she knew this behaviour manifested in other areas of her life and was detrimental to realising her goals because of a need to be sure of the outcomes and have complete control over the intervening actions. While she initially projected this mindset through the resources, the ensuing discussion enabled Alex to explore the real issue and consider resolutions.

Well-Being

Many clients consider coaching with collage as 'time for me' because they know that working with this approach is likely to elicit enjoyment and relaxation (Baqaeen, 2018). Furthermore, depending on the choice between the classic or digital option, an initial 1-1 coaching session lasts between two to three hours, reinforcing this sense of time out. The length and nature of the first two stages of the process are designed to help clients slow down. With this change of pace, there is a greater focus on the task at hand as they become fully immersed in gathering images and then creating their collage. This immersion engenders flow and mindfulness, explaining why the CCT is frequently described in the following manner, "I have found the session hugely relaxing," and "That felt therapeutic, like an emotional spa." These experiences help promote a sense of well-being, so although not developed as an 'Arts for Health and Well-being'[17] tool, as an arts-based process, it nevertheless facilitates similar results achieved with those approaches. Research conducted on the CCT confirms well-being as an outcome, both in the short and long term (Baqaeen, 2018). The immediate benefits are attributed to experiencing mindfulness and flow. Longer-term ones relate to coaching with collage developing clients personal awareness and fostering resilience and acceptance, which contributes to well-being through "increased self-regulation of emotions and behaviours in response to situations or stressors at work" (Baqaeen, 2018, p. 27). These findings were based on outcomes from research participants interviewed up to three years after creating their collages. While the study focused on work, previous and subsequent client feedback testify to these beneficial outcomes and the longevity of this impact across all areas of life. Therefore, as a coaching tool, in engendering a state of well-being, the CCT increases the possibility of clients achieving their goals and aspirations despite situations they find challenging or stressful.

Flow, Mindfulness, and Art-Making

Flow, mindfulness, and art-making share the following attributes that facilitate a client's sense of well-being:

- focused attention on an activity
- outside distractions receding
- a diminished sense of the self-conscious ego
- easing access to the unconscious and intuitive mind
- experiencing time differently – usually as passing faster
- engendering relaxation, enjoyment and a sense of fulfilment

Flow state, art-making, and mindfulness also enhance creativity as an individual's capacity for divergent thinking improves due to increased levels of attentiveness and enjoyment (Baqaeen, 2018; Fogo, 2017; Loudon & Deininger, 2017).

Flow

Mihaly Csikszentmihalyi developed the concept of flow, defining it as "the mental state of operation in which a person performing an activity is fully immersed in a feeling of energised focus, full involvement and enjoyment in the activity" (Csikszentmihalyi, 1990, p. 35). He describes this flow state as an optimal experience, requiring an element of achievable challenge. Furthermore, like mindfulness and art-making, individuals effectively disregard unwanted stimulation by remaining focused on what is relevant during the activity. For clients, this means giving their full attention to steadily look through the magazines and removing images before concentrating on composing their collage. Although this process is effortless from a practical perspective, clients remain engaged, absorbed, and curious because of the intensely personal nature of the activity and images. Hence time seems to fly. The challenge arises in retaining this focus when cognitive thoughts try to intrude. However, by adopting a mindful approach of noticing but disregarding these ruminations, clients can remain in a flow state.

Mindfulness

The description of mindfulness is, "Moment-to-moment, non-judgmental awareness, cultivated by paying attention in a specific way, that is, in the present moment, and as non-reactively, as non-judgementally, and as openheartedly as possible" (Kabat-Zinn, 2015, p. 1). Other definitions also include remaining curious. These requirements, especially remaining non-judgemental, open, and curious, are essential to arts-based methodologies. With the CCT, adopting these attitudes enables the client to be with what emerges as they create their collage without self-criticism concerning its aesthetics. To facilitate this type of engagement, the coach ensures the client is aware that their composition will not be scrutinised or assessed.[5] Instead, its intended purpose is a tool for personal visual expression and communication. This knowledge significantly reduces clients' concerns around perceptions of failure, relieving any pressure to perform (Loudon & Deininger, 2017). Consequently, this lowers self-conscious feelings, allowing the client to relax, enjoy the activity and engage fully.

From a well-being perspective, numerous studies, including Brown & Ryan (2003), evidence the link between mindfulness and an increase in a positive emotional state, as well as a reduction in negativity. Equally, research into the health benefits of art-making demonstrates its efficacy in decreasing stress and anxiety by lowering cortisol levels and increasing positive feelings through visual expression, which activates the brain's reward pathway (Kaimal et al., 2016). As a result of these neurological processes, the client's perception of the art-making experience is pleasurable, engendering the enjoyment and fulfilment that fosters well-being.

Resolving Inner Conflict

As they approach coaching, clients often come with assumptions concerning their session, namely, around their goals and the nature of what holds them back. Invariably, they usually discover the focus of their concerns is a symptom and not the cause of their challenge, discontent, unhappiness, or struggle. This revelation occurs as the unconscious mind surfaces the true source of the obstruction, most commonly an inner conflict.

These images express a sense of readiness to move forward while simultaneously being held back, masked, or contained. This duality may be present within one image, as in Trinity's and Astrid's client reflections. Or appear across two, as was the case in 'The Authors Story.' Whichever form they take, they enable clients to consider the gap between their current and future self, including mindset, goals, and behaviours.

The source of their struggle may result from internalised societal expectations, the head versus the heart decisions, unforgiveness of their past behaviours, not having a voice, or separating their identity into compartments. Examples of this are an MA Political Science graduate expressing conflict about enjoying gaming and a nightclub owner questioning how that aligns with their spiritual business. The belief that specific behaviours, attitudes, and interests are diametrically opposed and fixed ideas of right or wrong cause anxiety, guilt, and uncertainty that prevents clients from freely enjoying life and moving purposefully towards their goals. Regardless of where the internal conflict originates, working with the unconscious and collage effectively brings these mindsets, emotions, and unresolved pasts to the client's attention.

The paper acts as a container, holding these contradictions visually as the coach supports the client to work with any confusion. In this space, the collage reveals the truth of their 'stuckness,' enabling clients to witness and name the conflict rather than battling it intern-ally. Moreover, seeing their seemingly disparate thoughts and feelings co-exist in a physical space allows clients to appreciate the possibility of them being present in their life without being a source of psychological discord. With this shift in mindset comes an immediate acceptance of duality that empowers them to be with things as they are. Consequently, clients can redirect their energy to fulfilling their potential rather than focusing on the angst and stress caused by internal conflict. This transformation is illustrated below and in other case studies and client reflections throughout the book.

Client Reflections | On Resolving Inner Conflict

Trinity chose to work with me about her future, particularly career change, as she felt stuck and uncertain. The following reflection focuses on the image in the bottom right corner of two women in suits on an unusual red chair. This image proved to be crucial as a catalyst for change.

"As I looked through a tech magazine, I was astonished to have a visceral reaction from a mundane image of a weird chair someone was trying to sell! I didn't know that this image was going to say stuff because when I put it down, I was genuinely like, 'why Trinity? this is such a weird chair.' That's all that was going on in my head. Then as soon as we started talking about it, it brought up the core thing that I've been struggling with, so that was pretty amazing. This chair held the battle between my future and the past that was holding me back. Feeling like two different people, the lady sitting on top represents

Figure 9.2.1 Trinity's collage.

the mistakes I'd made in the past. The other was my future, the more rounded person. At first this image reflected my sense of, 'Oh I seem to be faking being half decent because I keep making these mistakes and that can't be right,' and 'when's it going to happen again?' I was so caught up in the idea of doing it right. So, there was this battle between how I saw myself and how I wanted to be.

Reflecting on the lady at the front with her shoes off, I came to realise 'that can be who you are,' in the sense that my identity isn't defined by my mistakes. I can choose how I feel about and view myself, instead of thinking 'this person keeps messing up.' I accepted that, actually, we all make mistakes, and that doesn't take away from trying to be the best person you can be, which was a core thing. The realisation that 'you are enough' was pretty much instantaneous then. It was just the most profound thing to come to the realisation that you are a sum of all the parts and that you may not like what you've done, but you can forgive yourself. That's why I think I put the lady on the circle wobbly chair, on top of the section of my collage that's about my future, knowing I can go forward reconciled to my past.

The collage returned me to my sense of self and the confidence I used to have in who I was as a person, which the mistakes had slowly eroded away. This is probably where my change started because I learned that I was able to let go of the internal monologue a little bit which then increased my joy and allowed me to go and try new things. The other stuff was a natural progression of me growing from having done the collage. So, step-by-step these were the areas I focused on. The first was job satisfaction. I was free to go and try that, and then I recognised I would like to do something to improve my physicality, seen in the little clay figure who looks playful and is enjoying their body.

Looking back, I can see my collage made an impact. Amazing things have happened with work and learning to love what my body can do." (Trinity)

Constructivism

Constructivism is Jean Piaget's theory of learning, which states that individuals build knowledge structures based on their experience of the world (Hein, 1991; Rasmussen Consulting, 2012). His work emphasised the significance of an individual's active role in constructing meaning by exploring their life stories. Piaget saw it as a narrative process where learning evolves only through new experiences being assimilated and made sense of in relation to existing ones. In this way, individuals continually construct their identity as they learn. As such, constructivists argue that knowledge is not independent of a learner or the meaning they ascribe to their experiences. Furthermore, the way people perceive the world results from the self-generated thoughts originating in their personally constructed knowledge (Hein, 1991). These constructs become 'the stories we tell ourselves,' and the identities clients consequently adopt.

Constructionism

First coined by Seymour Papert, the term constructionism emerged from constructivism but holds that learning happens most effectively when people are also actively constructing something external to themselves (Ackermann, 2001; Rasmussen Consulting, 2012). Papert's theory asserts that through the act of creating something in the real world, the individual is simultaneously constructing internal knowledge in their mind. Furthermore, abstract information such as emotions and values become visual and tangible, enabling them to be more readily understood. These learning theories acknowledge that learning it not simply an accumulation of knowledge.

The Hand and Mind Connection

Studies in archaeology and palaeontology shed light on the connection between the hand and mind and the critical role of this association in human development. First discovered by Mary and Louis Leakey, this link resulted from the evolutionary necessity to construct and use tools (Marchand, 2012). The body of research in this area encompasses such disciplines as anatomy, physiology, neuroscience, and anthropology. These sciences support the premise that the hand and mind work collaboratively, informing and learning from the other rather than either being a dominant influence (Jones, 2006; Rich, 1999). Essentially, the consensus is that the hand and mind are inseparable.

The extent of this co-dependency is seen in the models of the cortical homunculus.[18] Based on a neurological map, these distorted figures reflect the areas and proportions of the brain dedicated to processing motor and sensory functions. Developed by Wilder Penfield and Edwin Boldrey, the models, with their disproportionally large hands and lips, clearly illustrate how the hands' sensory and motor nerves cover large areas of the brain, indicative of the strong connection between them.

Just as the prevalence of visual stimuli means the influence of images is often overlooked, so too are the hands and the integral part they play in learning alongside cognitive reasoning. Nonetheless, psychologists and biologists are recognising that the visual arts inherently tap this evolutionary trait that enables people to learn by making (Judkins, 2014). The hands are "the most effective body part for manipulating objects … communicating, expressing, and even shaping ideas and emotions" (Marchand, 2012, p. 261). Therefore, it is unsurprising that when artists use theirs, they intuitively explore possibilities, evaluate emotions, and develop ideas whilst creating.

As an arts-based method (ABM), the CCT allows clients to experience and benefit from an approach facilitating this synchronicity between hand and mind. When clients create their coaching collage, the mind leads the hand, and vice versa, stimulating the other into action until the image arrangement intuitively feels right and makes sense cognitively. Guidance from the coach to notice their internal analysing, questioning, and integration of ideas, feelings, and concepts ensure clients attain deeper awareness and clarity as hand and mind knowledge converge.

Constructing the Collage

Based on these theories, clients benefit from reflecting and engaging in meaning-making by exploring their lived experiences as they construct their collage. Predominantly symbolic and metaphorical, their images capture the client's often complex experiences that impact and inform meaning-making around their chosen theme. Furthermore, rather than concretely presenting information, the client's visual metaphors allude to and imply meaning based on intuitive knowing (Barner, 2011). From a constructionist perspective, this form of knowledge is valuable because it tangibly expresses their reality in an emotional and meaningful way. In originating from the unconscious, this imagery also elicits forgotten or hidden material pertinent to how clients define themselves that they may otherwise exclude while reconstructing their identity.

Client Reflections | On Reconstructing Identity

"I attended a public workshop with the theme of clarity and confidence and had expected to create a completely different collage. I was surprised at the number of words that resonated. The number seventeen was the first image that I pulled out and it took my breath away. I was shocked that I'd had such a reaction to it, it wasn't as though I hadn't seen the number many times before. It represented a traumatic event.

The number seventeen unconsciously shaped the rest of the collage. I knew I'd begin with it, and everything else flowed from that. It wouldn't have made sense to put positive words next to it, so all the dark words are around it, as is the small image that looks like a mannequin. The outer layer of clothing looks really uncomfortable with loads of strapping that's tight and restrictive. It reflects how I felt I had to hide my feelings, what happened, and how I felt really changed.

The 'dark matter' is a tiny bit in the corner. The rest is me moving, growing, finding, creating, and travelling. Most is positive, that's what I see in it, encouraging myself. I'd felt detached and not myself, but the words 'home' and 'belonging' show me otherwise. When I finished, I realised something had happened in that moment of creating the collage. I was excited to share it, I wanted to let it out. I wasn't afraid to say, 'something traumatic happened to me at the age of seventeen.' I wouldn't have been able to say that before, let alone to a group of strangers, it would have been a trigger, yet I could say it now.

I only saw the processing, growth, and journey I'd been on from that event reflected in the collage. It's like an embodiment of my journey from the 'beginners guide to dark

Figure 9.2.2 Chidiebube collage.

matter,' and 'secrets,' to 'liberated,' 'love,' and 'you are my light on the horizon.' The experience was very strange, it almost felt like God's hand. It profoundly changed how I see myself as a person, and because of that, it changed how I see the world, moving me forward in a massive way when I hadn't even realised I was stuck. It helped me see I am not that event, so I don't need to be fearful because I've been on a journey and will continue to be, towards light and love and not darkness. That gives me hope for the future, and that's liberating.

I felt the traumatic event that happened when I was seventeen covered my authentic self. In that event, I thought I'd forever lost the person I could have been. Because for years I had been grieving for that version of myself, I had felt constrained. I missed her and the potential of her, but through the collage, I realised she wasn't gone, I found myself. I understood that the seventeen-year-old me is not a separate entity from the woman I am now, and the event does not define me. It was like an awakening and that's what I named my collage. Now, every time I look at it, it reminds me that I'm still here and I'm still me. In finding myself, I want to know what I can do, who I can be because the version where I saw myself as separate from the girl before the event hadn't been working. She was entirely different to who I was created to be. One change I've made is in how I dress. Although I have always loved colour, for a long time I used to wear dark clothes because I was trying to hide. Now I am happy to be seen, so enjoy wearing the vibrant colours which are true to who I am.

I've always flicked through the pages of magazines and never thought they would say anything to me. I just looked at them on a superficial level and can't believe I found the things I wanted to say in a magazine. But actually, it almost felt like the images found me. Being able to manipulate the images to say what I wanted to say was empowering and interesting. For example, 'Transform the legacy,' I created that, a very real action of manipulating and changing things to express something about me, moulding and creating. Importantly, I was in control of what had felt out of control. This sense of control extended to deciding how much I'd disclose.

I love how the collage looks. For someone who does not consider themselves artistic, creating something that I find beautiful and can put on my wall is a joy. I think, 'I did this' and it has a personal meaning that speaks to me and continues to have a powerful and profound impact on my life. I love that." (Chidiebube)

Gathering it Together

The theories and information in this chapter section focus on expressions of 'self' available through the creative coaching process involving working with magazines, while some, such as projection, occur on an unconscious level. Others are a result of conscious decisions and may offer transferable learning opportunities beyond the coaching session. As an approach that includes an art-making element, the CCT enriches clients' self-expression through engendering flow and mindfulness and promoting well-being. These three outcomes facilitate a deeper connection to the unconscious because of reduced censorship and judgement, enabling authentic self-expression. Consequently, a significant benefit to clients is revealing the truth of their blocks through an external, visually tangible object that allows them to explore the issue and seek resolutions. Crucially, the hand and mind connection facilitates an empowering expression of 'self,' as clients reconstruct their identity while creating their collage.

Bibliography

Ackermann, E. (2001). *Piaget's Constructivism, Papert's Constructionism: What's the difference?* www. sylviastipich.com/wp-content/uploads/2015/04/Coursera-Piaget-_-Papert.pdf

Baqaeen, L. (2018). *Mindfulness in the art-making for employee well-being: An exploratory study on collage.* City, University of London.

Barner, R. W. (2011). Applying visual metaphors to career transitions. *Journal of Career Development, 38*(1), 89–106. https://doi.org/10.1177/0894845309359287

Branthwaite, A. (2002). Investigating the power of imagery in marketing communication: Evidence-based techniques. *Qualitative Market Research: An International Journal, 5*(3), 164–171. https://doi.org/10.1108/13522750210432977

Brown, K. W., & Ryan, R. M. (2003). The Benefits of Being Present: Mindfulness and Its Role in Psychological Well-Being. *Journal of Personality and Social Psychology, 84*(4), 822–848. https://doi.org/10.1037/0022-3514.84.4.822

Colakoglu, S., & Littlefield, J. (2011). Teaching Organizational Culture Using a Projective Technique: Collage Construction. *Journal of Management Education, 35*(4), 564–585. https://doi.org/10.1177/1052562910390315

Csikszentmihalyi, M. (1990). *Flow: The Psychology of Optimal Experience.* Harper & Row.

Fitzpatrick, L. (2014). *The Cycle of Creativity: Gestalt Coaching and the Creative Process.* Gestalt Review. https://doi.org/10.5325/gestaltreview.18.2.0161

Fogo, L. G. (2017). *Engagement with the Visual Arts Increases Mindfulness* [University of Tennessee at Chattanooga, United States]. http://scholar.utc.edu/honors-theses

Hein, G. E. P. (Lesley C. M. U. (1991). Constructivist Learning Theory. *Constructivist Learning Theory: The Museum and the Needs of People.* https://doi.org/10.4135/9781412972024.n523

Jones, E. G. (2006). The sensory hand. *Brain, 129*(12), 3413–3420. https://doi.org/10.1093/brain/awl308

Judkins, R. (2014). *Think With Your Hands | Psychology Today.* Psychology Today. www.psychologyto day.com/us/blog/connect-creativity/201408/think-your-hands

Kabat-Zinn, J. (2015). Mindfulness. *Mindfulness, 6*(6), 1481–1483. https://doi.org/10.1007/s12 671-015-0456-x

Kaimal, G., Ray, K., & Muniz, J. (2016). Reduction of Cortisol Levels and Participants' Responses Following Art Making. *Art Therapy, 33*(2), 74–80. https://doi.org/10.1080/07421 656.2016.1166832

Loudon, G. H., & Deininger, G. M. (2017). The Physiological Response to Drawing and Its Relation to Attention and Relaxation. *Journal of Behavioral and Brain Science, 07*(03), 111–124. https://doi.org/10.4236/jbbs.2017.73011

Malchiodi, C. (Ed.). (2003). *Handbook of Art Therapy* (Vol. 31, Issue 3). Guildford Press. https://doi.org/10.1016/j.aip.2004.03.002

Marchand, T. H. (2012). Knowledge in Hand: Explorations of Brain, Hand and Tool. In *Handbook of Social Anthropology* (pp. 260–269). Sage. https://visa2013.sciencesconf.org/conference/visa2 013/pages/Marchand_2012.pdf

Martin, L., & Schwartz, D. L. (2014). A pragmatic perspective on visual representation and creative thinking. *Visual Studies, 29*(1), 80–93. https://doi.org/10.1080/1472586X.2014.862997

Porr, C., Mayan, M., Graffigna, G., Wall, S., & Vieira, E. R. (2011). The Evocative Power of Projective Techniques for the Elicitation of Meaning. *International Journal of Qualitative Methods, 10*(1), 30–41. https://doi.org/10.1177/160940691101000103

Rasmussen Consulting. (2012). *The Science Behind the LEGO SERIOUS PLAY method.*

Rich, G. J. (1999). The Hand: How Its Use Shapes the Brain, Language, and Human Culture: The Hand: How Its Use Shapes the Brain, Language, and Human Culture. *Anthropology of Consciousness, 10*(1), 62–64. https://doi.org/10.1525/ac.1999.10.1.62

PART 3 | CREATIVITY IN PRACTICE

Play

For many adults, play is viewed strictly as a child's activity. Consequently, it is underrated and dismissed as frivolous, pointless, and a waste of time (Brown, 2009). Left behind in childhood, many individuals lose the valuable benefits of continuing this activity. However, understanding its contribution to creativity, problem-solving, and building confidence encourages clients to appreciate and actively reconnect with the joy of playing.

The Purpose of Play

According to Brown (2009), play is imperative, fuelling creativity, innovation, and the expression of personal truths. He describes it as critical to happiness, relationships, and productivity. In recognising the freedom, emotions, and possibilities evoked by play, Brown advocates it for its own sake. Rasmussen Consulting (2012) propose that when adults play, it is always with a sense of their identity, encompassing ideas, emotions, and cognition without editing or censoring by themselves or others.

From a neurological perspective, research shows play as having an active role in releasing endorphins, improving brain functionality, promoting creativity, and stimulating the prefrontal cortex where executive decisions are made (Brown, 2009). In the CCT, the roles of play and creativity[19] interconnect when clients create their collage. During this activity, play is the mechanism for reorganising existing and new information together in unfamiliar ways that lead to solutions, meaning-making, and resolutions. This process is essential to client learning, psychological growth, insights, and the decision making that supports their coaching aims.

Permission to Play

Art-making is fundamentally a form of play and, akin to art, is outside of many clients' usual activities. Therefore, when a client undertakes coaching with the CCT, play is another unfamiliar aspect of the technique that increases the potential to access new information.[20]

The word 'play' is used to introduce the second stage of the CCT. This language encapsulates the attributes of collage creation and consequently helps clients understand the attitude and approach to take when making theirs. Accordingly, this time is an opportunity to embrace curiosity, trial and error, risk-taking, and a willingness to remain open to possibilities. Internal questions such as, "What if?" and "What happens when?" stimulate this playful approach, which is reinforced by the coach, who emphasises that they cannot do it wrong. In accepting this, clients give themselves permission to move away from rigid behaviours, accepted mindsets, and formal learning structures. Consequently, play means clients approaching coaching without fixed ideas of their next steps. While working with the unknown is not comfortable for everyone, ultimately adopting a mindset of play is freeing, removes pressure and ensures that client's responses, conclusions, and choices are not arrived at prematurely.

Just as the word 'art' can act as a barrier to client engagement, so can 'play.' In these instances, coaches can adjust their language slightly and confirm clients understand its meaning in the context of coaching with a creative tool. Alternative suggestions are creative or purposeful play.

While understanding the power of play for self-development, it is equally relevant to remember it is inherently enjoyable. This outcome is important because when clients enjoy the coaching experience, it increases their energy level, engagement in the process, and ability to stay with the more challenging aspects of the process for longer.

External Visualisation

In coaching, visualisation usually refers to the internal process of mentally forming an image. To keep this vision alive, clients must keep replaying and refreshing it. In contrast, by constructing their collage as a tangible object, clients use external visualisation where thoughts, values, emotions, experiences, and beliefs are represented physically as images. In this state, they are available as objects for reflection and comparison, manipulation and reintegration (Martin & Schwartz, 2014).

The process is a self-directed experience as clients edit, organise, rearrange, and adjust their gathered images while creating their collage. The action of literally moving their experiences, emotions, values, and so forth into a variety of different positions on the card allows relationships, connections, and patterns between often seemingly disparate images to emerge. These associations appear, for example, through image content, colour, shape, and positioning as they merge in clusters, layers, and flows. Effectively, this activity reorganises information from the unconscious to facilitate meaning-making as the client's collage composition generates the coherent form and structure that cognition seeks. As a creative technique, the executive attention network[1] reflects, questions, reviews, analyses, and clarifies existing concepts and beliefs each time images are moved or adjusted. Consequently, the opportunity to play with their internal processing in an external landscape enables clients to notice themselves; their mindsets, emotions, and behaviours reflected visually in the content and layout of their narrative.

Client Reflections | On Noticing the 'Self'

"I find my collage really confusing. But I think that's because I've got lots of ideas about my next steps, but they're all jumbled up in my mind and I've been unable to separate them. I also think there are no white spaces between the images because everything feels chaotic and jumbled. At least now I can see it all on paper." (Matthew)

"I like things to feel orderly and controlled. That's why everything is cut out so neatly and placed in separate sections. The white space means I can see things clearly, which is comforting. The only problem is, I know that I don't take risks and try new things because that feels messy and unpredictable. Maybe that's why my collage is so neat." (Sarah)

"The collage appears positive. The words are joyful, purposeful with a 'can do' attitude, yet when I put it together, I realised I wasn't. This wasn't the discovery of my drive; this was a revelation that I feel overwhelmed, even by things that are not essentially bad. What it revealed in its busyness to me, was how much I try to cram into my pandemic reduced capacity. My collage helped me see I require more stillness." (Teresa)

Working with White Space

Two of these reflections include references to the white space in the collage. By clarifying what they represent for clients or the feelings they engender, these 'gaps,' or lack of them, can provide as much information as an image. Frequent client interpretations are space to breathe, allowing room for anything to happen, stillness, and emptiness. Sometimes, clients express discomfort at leaving white spaces and attempt to fill them. This reaction offers further opportunities for client discovery and meaning-making, elicited through coaching questions. Significantly, these visible areas of the card only materialise as a source of exploration because of external visualisation.

Reconstructing Identity

Clients can also safely test how it might be and feel for them to experience alternative scenarios and desired outcomes by removing or expanding, disassembling and combining, reshaping and repositioning images to reflect these possibilities (Malchiodi, 2003). This trialling includes literally seeing things from a different perspective by changing the direction of the card from portrait to landscape and back again, exploring how the images fit and flow, before settling on an orientation. Another method of conveying potential versions of themselves is by changing the size and shape of the card, which is usually a result of clients collaging over the edges. This decision is described by many as a deliberate choice to expand their boundaries and comfort zone. Colour also has a role in personal expression and suggesting ways of being. When significant to clients, it emanates in their images and, like everything they present, is explored to determine their unique interpretation. Crucially, in the act of altering their images or composition, clients literally and figuratively reshape their thinking, either reinforcing those models that serve them well or transforming unhelpful mindsets. Martin & Schwartz (2014, p. 83) wrote of this as an outcome in stating that "Opportunities for reinterpretation can be especially powerful when elements of the visualisation can be moved or rearranged." Whichever way they choose to play with their sense of identity and emotional expressions, when clients explore for the sake of discovery, they create something new and change the perception of what they can accomplish. This experience is both challenging and liberating.

Client Case Study

Freda chose to work with me because she felt stuck and uncertain about the future, particularly relating to her current career. She struggled with a role where she felt undermined and unappreciated while also facing the risk of redundancy. As a result, her confidence and self-esteem were negatively affected, leaving her fearful concerning the future. Freda felt a strong resonance with an image of a woman entering a dark room. The photo was taken from the perspective of someone standing in the room looking at the woman. As she pushed the door wide open, the only light came from behind her so that she stood silhouetted in the doorway. Freda found this image challenging, describing it as reflecting her current situation of entering a state where things were unknown and in darkness. She shared the meaning of the image with me before completing her collage. During the conversation, in seeing the image from an alternative perspective, Freda experienced an a-ha moment. Rather than stepping into a dark room, she saw herself as opening the door and letting the light flood in, a perceptual shift she described as empowering. In response to this internal reframe, she literally and figuratively chose to cut away the darkness, leaving the woman standing silhouetted in the open doorway.[21] In her completed collage, this image is central, with images of nature and positive affirmations replacing the darkness.

Figure 9.3.1 Freda's collage.

With increased confidence and self-belief in her ability to affect personal change, Freda found alternative employment before she was made redundant.

Enriching Projection

As an arts-based method (ABM), every aspect of the CCT involves an outward expression of the 'self.' Therefore, how clients work with their images enriches the projective quality of the technique, in that images are altered to reflect the emotions they associate with the content. For instance, tearing engenders a different meaning to cutting. Numerous clients describe their torn edges as creating a sense of softness. In response to the question, "What kind of softness?", the answers are frequently "freedom," "spontaneity," "pleasant," and "enjoyable." These 'softer' edges also appear as corners rounded with scissors. Conversely, angular pointed corners generally elicit the following descriptions "order," "regimented," "firm," and "hard." Collective language patterns such as these become apparent through an accumulation of coaching client's individual interpretations.

Clients often feel compelled to work with their images in a certain way stating, "I had to make it circular because I wanted everything to feel softer, kinder." Or, "It didn't feel right tearing it." Whether a conscious or unconscious response, how clients engage with the image can deepen their cognitive awareness of its meaning. This was aptly illustrated by an individual at a group coaching session on well-being who said, "I surprised myself by how carefully I cut this word out, I had no idea how important what it represents is to me. Now I realise that perhaps it's too important, as I give so much of myself to it, potentially at the cost of my well-being." (Michael)

Embodied Cognition

Besides its role as a remembered physical experience that enables learning through metaphors,[22] embodiment allows opportunities for immediate acquisition of sensory knowledge during collage creation. This understanding results from the physical experience of clients working with their hands or using scissors as an extension of their hands. In the scenario above, Michael was completely aware of his physical movements as he exercised control and care whilst cutting out the image. The nature of his immediate embodied response to the contents in the image informed his internal processing, leading to enhanced self-awareness. Foglia & Wilson (2013) explain this phenomenon as the body supporting cognition by taking on information to streamline cognitive functions. Essentially, 'lightening the load' on conscious thinking means tasks such as problem-solving, using the imagination, and remembering are more effective.

Furthermore, the body is also pivotal as clients reject or retain specific images. Sometimes the rejection is a way of saying

"No!" with the physical act of discarding the image a powerful statement of intent. As a contrasting declaration, when clients securely glue their images into position, these deliberate movements affirm ownership of their story, its meaning, and intentions.

Client Reflections | On Letting Go

"As important as what did make it into my final collage, were the images I discarded. I had just come out of a very difficult and stressful work environment and one of the first images I found was of Shrek, that I connected with my old boss who had been such a negative factor in my life for some time. Originally intending to place 'him' in the collage to remind me what I would not put up with any longer; I found myself able to decide, by the end of the process, that I did not in fact need him there after all. This has served as a useful mental visualisation any time I need to be reminded of where I have come from, and where I am going." (Nicola)

"The perfume bottle represents perfection to me. I recognise that I am a perfectionist and want to change this, that's why I've left it off my collage. But I have included a picture of the child on swing because it reminds me that I want to have fun and give myself permission to play more. I feel my life is too stifled and I don't want to feel like that anymore." (Jennifer)

As the architect of their collage composition, the decision to exclude or include elements of their current story empowers clients. Witnessed by the coach, these choices, embodied while constructing their narrative, are the client's first active steps towards achieving the change they seek.

Positioning

The role of the image is paramount in meaning-making; however, their position on the card and relative to each other also offers significant insight and the ability to create shifts for clients. Although no two collages are ever the same, repeated patterns emerge around compositions and the collective meaning clients assign to these layouts. If they do not see a pattern themselves, the coach's awareness of those that hold a collective meaning allows them to notice on the client's behalf. This information is valuable in enabling clients to check resonance and potentially attain deeper insight. It can never be used to interpret or make assumptions. Therefore, as with archetypal symbols, to elicit personal understanding, exploration of clients' image placement occurs after they share their collage and during the coaching conversation. Until then, there is no indication which layout, if any, is present. For this reason, the coach remains intrigued concerning what the composition might reveal as the story unfolds.

The following themes are based on the most frequently recurring layouts:

The Book

The 'book' is one of the most frequently occurring themes and is so named because the collage is like the pages of an open book, read from left to right and associated with turning a page.[23] Here, a client positions and describes the images in two sections indicative of a transition from past to present, or more usually present and future. With the latter, the left-hand side reflects their current situation, emotions, and so forth, while the right features the changes they seek to create and experience. This split is rarely definitive, and one or two images concerning the past regularly appear on the side relating to what lies ahead and vice versa. The content of these images helps clients understand the connection between their history and their future, their aspirations and current perspectives. The 'book' layout often emerges when clients create their first collage.

The Trio

These collages are composed of three horizontal or vertical sections. In these bands, clients present and understand visual information as distinct segments or as a sequential occurrence. Generally, segments contain information related to the client's character traits, emotions, behaviours, and different areas of life, while sequences capture linear events or activities. Along the lines of the 'book,' in the 'trio' each section's content may overlap or, through the narrative, flow seamlessly from one part to another. With the latter, if this reflects recurring events or activities, these collages can help clients identify mindsets and behaviours at each stage of a process that either prevent or support them to move forward effectively. (See Figure 9.1.3 Nicholas' collage.)

The Tree

Without roots supporting and holding them firmly in place, trees will blow over easily in a storm; these root systems are also vital to their health. For this reason, the 'tree' describes when clients share how the images at the bottom of their collage represent the source of their strength, determination, love, focus, hope, motivation, and so forth. Every client's collection of 'tree roots' is different. Nonetheless, patterns surface, with images that represent values, beliefs, characteristics, skills, purpose, family, and friends frequently present. Clients speak of how everything else emerges from, or is built on, this foundation as they seek to achieve their goals and aspirations.

The River

Just as rivers meander in different directions, connected images flow across the card, moving up and down, side to side, and back around on themselves. Usually, the collage contains visual cues that guide the eye to see associations, such as colours, shapes, or similar content. (In this respect, the 'river' is the only collage that potentially indicates its layout prior to the storytelling). These visible similarities also connect through the meaning they hold. When the images do not appear linked, physically or visually, the client's narrative creates the flow, and the visual pattern becomes noticeable. Clients describe these collages in terms of seeing or seeking effortless movement from one thing to another, providing connections where they had not seen them. The whole collage may be a 'river' layout or specific images and words combine to run through.

Centre Stage

As the name implies, these collages feature a centrally positioned image. Instinctively, the eye is drawn here, and everything else radiates from and flows to this focal point. Appearing as a person, place, animal, or object, it comes in various sizes and is occasionally offset from the centre. It also emerges as a single word, phrase, sentence, or quote. Whatever form it takes, clients describe this image as a representation of their future self, and for this reason it projects a critical aspect of their identity. With an association to the archetypal symbol of the circle, these images hold the promise of a sense of completeness, explaining why they are always aspirational. Along with the 'book,' 'centre stage' layouts are the most frequently occurring compositions. (See Figure 2.1 The author's collage).

Yin and Yang

This layout refers to clients placing circumstances, experiences, and emotions that they find uncomfortable and challenging at the base of their collage and those that energise and fulfil them at the top. These positions correlate to up and down as orientational metaphors. As mentioned previously in Chapter 8, up is associated with happiness and more, conversely down is sad and less. Furthermore, clients may use the related language of uplifted and downcast when describing aspects of their collage. However, through exploration and discussion, like yin and yang, what first appear as opposites come to be understood as dualism. As this recognition shifts the client's understanding, it reduces inner conflict and engenders feelings of acceptance. (See Figure 14.1 Rosie's digital collage).

Other positions that are helpful for the coach to be aware of are potential anchor points and headlines. The former refers to the corners of the card, the latter to the top. Anchor points appear at one or more corners within a composition. These images hold significant meaning, impact, and power for clients and help them to maintain a steadfast attitude and focus when feeling de-motivated or facing challenges. Headlines are word(s) placed at the top of a collage as an affirmation, statement, or declaration of the client's goals or future identity.

"This Queen has no equal is an affirmation recognising who I am. I know God loves, likes, and holds me, even when I want to hide away." (Trinity) (See Figure 9.2.1 Trinity's collage).

Laying It All Out

The complexity of a client's circumstances, experiences, emotions, and desires means that even when a primary layout emerges, their collage is likely to feature more than one.

Moreover, a different theme to those described may surface, or none at all. Yet every composition contains a narrative, because while the collage paints an overall picture, micro-stories appear through image arrangement within the layout. Consequently, clients keep their whole story in view, while simultaneously incorporating and processing the individual elements it contains. Therefore, whether positioned unconsciously or consciously, all clients' image placements contribute valuable information for exploration, insights and meaning-making.

Questions to support elicitation of the meaning of layouts include:

- tell me about the layout
- what do you notice about where your images are positioned?
- does this resonate with you?
- why did you position [x] there?

Client Reflections | Collage Layout as a Metaphorical Journey

"My collage is about my journey from what I've been doing to where I want to go. I've got a small picture of a desk and a gold-encrusted shape on the left, representing how I have been provided for by God within the boundaries of working in an office. The blue represents thoughts that are the beginnings of something, while the green shoots are these things overtaking what I was doing before. They're growing and thriving with flowers at the end, germinating into something else."

Figure 9.3.2 Anwa's collage.

In the middle of my collage, I'm questioning myself, 'How am I going to do this? I don't want these boundaries, but how am I going to move from where I am to where I want to be?' I saw the picture of the astronaut who's running fast to get away from something. I like the fact that he's connected with space because it's something without limits. That's why that picture resonated with me. The windows and white bubbles reflect my thoughts. If I couldn't get out to the countryside, I'd sit near the window and look out, opening up the opportunity to draw inspiration from outside to overcome things enclosing me.

The last part is a watercolour. That resonated because it merged all of these thoughts together to come up with something that looks really beautiful. Marrying who I am, with what I want to do without having to be one way at work, another way at home or out on the street and then someone else at church. I could just be myself and that would be reflected in my career, where I could say, 'This is what I do.' So, the watercolour represents me being myself. Then at the bottom, the words sum up my journey' I was lost and now I'm found.'

My collage helped me visualise and understand the conflict that was going on within me. To put it down on paper meant I could understand it better. It was a bit of a release for me actually because I could see where I was and where I'm going. Since completing my collage, I've inquired about a childcare course that I'm waiting to start. I've also started voluntary work in that sector and am just really taking active steps towards achieving my goals." (Anwa)

The Collage | An Ongoing Coaching Resource

External visualisation ensures the information garnered during a client's experience coaching with the CCT is permanently available in the collage. Subsequently, accepting that images influence behaviour, as a resource their collage is a powerful tool for inspiring and motivating action. To ensure clients gain the most benefit from its potential to generate such outcomes, they are encouraged to place their collage as a personal primer,[24] where it can be regularly seen. A client's comments in the weeks after their coaching session illustrates the value in this. "I look at my collage every day and seem to find a different section or text to focus on each time, which takes on more meaning and relevance as each day passes. I feel inspired to achieve so much." (Karen).

Significantly, the images that resonate with individuals are a product of their interaction with the world. Consequently, they are dynamic, being brought to life by the meaning attributed to them and subject to reinterpretation or loss of influence as clients, or their situations, change.[25] Therefore, collages are valuable baselines for reflection and reviewing progress with clients. For this reason, the date is discreetly recorded, usually on the back.

Accountability

Coaches do not keep collages on a client's behalf because they are profoundly intimate with a critical role in empowering action and providing ongoing meaning and revelations. Fortunately, the pride, excitement, curiosity, and other emotions concerning their visual narrative ensure most clients take ownership of their collage, figuratively and literally. With the client's permission, the coach records a digital copy instead. In the rare case where a client requests the coach keep it, this becomes another area for discussion and exploration. Ultimately, the client remains responsible for their collage, so the coach follows the best practice of not retaining it even in these situations. The reason for this concerns maintaining boundaries as clients project aspects of the 'self' into their collage. Therefore, they would effectively leave a part of themselves with the coach to look after, rather than accepting accountability for the collage and, in turn, potentially themselves.

Co-creating with Clients

When coaching individuals with the CCT, co-creating[26] refers to being in the same space, involved in the first two arts-based stages of the process alongside the client. Sharing this experience has value whether face-to-face in a physical environment or delivering online.

Rather than a client creating a collage independently in preparation for coaching, the CCT requires that a coach guides them through the process during the session. Taking this approach is best practice and ensures the coach is present to notice physiological, emotional, and other learning opportunities on the client's behalf. Furthermore, working in this way establishes a sense of equality between client and coach, helping to build trust and openness. The activation of mirror neurons may also play a role in the development of the client and coach relationship. These are triggered when an activity is observed or understood, but they also activate when undertaking the same action as others (Foglia & Wilson, 2013). The benefits of these neurons include engendering a physical state that supports empathy and connection to others. Therefore, in the context of co-creating, it corroborates the value of this method of coaching. Crucially, creating this equal and open dynamic between client and coach lowers the client's self-consciousness, a state that improves access to their unconscious. Numerous clients attest to enjoying and appreciating this way of working, describing it as making them feel at ease. "It's really nice that Andréa sat and also did the same activities. I think this made the session much more comfortable." (Krisztina)

Should the coach not partake in the creative process, this could prove uncomfortable for both parties and potentially feel intimidating for the client. Nevertheless, during the activity it is imperative coaches always remain aware, attentive, and available to support the client as they gather images and create their collage. Therefore, coaches do not become fully absorbed in the process or enter a state of mindfulness or flow. Instead, they work consciously. Additionally, to ensure the focus remains entirely on the client, the coach neither completes their collage nor shares their images.

Co-creating is only recommended when coaching individuals, with agreement sought from them in advance of their session. It is unnecessary during group coaching because clients create alongside each other, and the coach must remain observant and aware of all members.

Culminating in a Collage

Even from a practical perspective, as clients construct their collages, creativity can never be divorced from cognition. Therefore, as they play, clients are engaged in a thought-provoking, insightful, and evaluative experience. This activity provides multiple learning opportunities while simultaneously capturing their story, hopes, and ambitions through the artistic expression found in the medium of collage. External and visual, as a foundation for them to build and embody the future they desire, clients create for themselves a uniquely personalised and powerful gift.

Notes

1 Bold type added for emphasis by the author.
2 For readers interested in learning more about this topic, substantial literature is available
3 See Chapter 7 | Coaching with the Unconscious.
4 Because of the level of personal dedication and time required, coaching with collage is not intended to support progress to Pro or Big-C. Moreover, some clients may already exhibit these types of creativity.
5 See Chapters 11 and 13 for in depth guidance on introducing an arts-based method to individuals and groups.
6 See Chapter 6 | The Power of Visual Communication.
7 When coaching with collage, the goal of the session is determined by the chosen theme.
8 See Chapter 8 | Part 1: Symbols and Metaphors for Meaning-making and Self-Awareness.
9 The term failure is used to acknowledge how clients may feel. However, in the context of coaching with collage, there is no concept of failure.
10 See Chapter 9 | Part 2: The Creative Process as an Expression of Self.
11 See Chapter 9 | Part 3: Creativity in Practice (Client Reflections).
12 See Chapter 14 | Coaching with Collage Online.
13 See Chapter 8 | Part 1: Symbols and Metaphors for Meaning-Making and Self-Awareness.
14 See Chapter 10 | Part 2: Storytelling in Groups (Reaching Resolutions).
15 See Chapter 6 | The Power of Visual Communication.
16 See Chapter 11 | Facilitating a Safe Space to Coach with a Creative Technique.
17 For more information on this subject see this all-party parliamentary inquiry report on the Arts for Health and Well-being https://ncch.org.uk/uploads/Creative_Health_Inquiry_Report_2017_-_Second_Edition.pdf.
18 An image of the models referred to can be found on Wikipedia via this link: https://images.app.goo.gl/9rJqczg4rVTwA1YJ6. They are on show at the Natural History Museum, London.
19 See Chapter 9 | Part 1: A Compelling Case for Creativity in Coaching.
20 See Chapter 6 | The Power of Visual Communication (Defamiliarising the Familiar).
21 Clara's collage includes a significant reference to archetypes, where the door represents transition. Additionally, with positioning 'herself' centrally she reflects the collective layout of Centre Stage.
22 See Chapter 8 | Part 1: Symbols and Metaphor for Meaning-Making and Self-Awareness (Embodiment).
23 There is recognition that this way of reading is not the same in every country or culture.
24 See Chapter 7 | Working with the Unconscious (The Collage as a Personal Primer).
25 See case study Figure 14.2.
26 The term co-creating is also used to describe the process whereby members of a group create a collaborative collage.

Bibliography

Brown, S. (2009). *Play*. Avery.
Foglia, L., & Wilson, R. (2017). *Embodied Cognition, The Stanford Encyclopedia of Philosophy.* https://plato.stanford.edu/archives/spr2017/entries/embodied-cognition/.

Foglia, L., & Wilson, R. A. (2013). Embodied cognition. *Wiley Interdisciplinary Reviews: Cognitive Science, 4*(3), 319–325. https://doi.org/10.1002/wcs.1226

Lakoff, G., & Johnson, M. (1980). *Metaphors We Live By.* The University of Chicago Press.

Malchiodi, C. (Ed.). (2003). *Handbook of Art Therapy* (Vol. 31, Issue 3). Guildford Press. https://doi.org/10.1016/j.aip.2004.03.002

Martin, L., & Schwartz, D. L. (2014). A pragmatic perspective on visual representation and creative thinking. *Visual Studies, 29*(1), 80–93. https://doi.org/10.1080/1472586X.2014.862997

Rasmussen Consulting. (2012). *The Science Behind the LEGO SERIOUS PLAY method.*

10 Storytelling and the Coaching Conversation

PART 1 | INDIVIDUAL STORYTELLING

Storytelling is essentially effective communication and, "There is not a culture on earth that does not tell, exchange, and enjoy stories," maintains Mighall (2013, p. 12). Through sharing, listening, remembering, and reflecting, stories help individuals make sense of the world and their place in it while simultaneously creating and preserving collective and personal history, which otherwise might be lost. Furthermore, as a means of communicating ideas, knowledge, thoughts, and feelings, stories allow emotional connections. For this reason, they engage and endure, deepening awareness of self and others in a way that fact-based information does not.

Storytelling for Emotional Connection | The Neuroscience

Neuroscience provides insight into what many people intuitively know- that stories can connect the storyteller and listener on an emotional level and that this is beneficial to both parties. According to Smith (2016), two hormones play a crucial role in this connection by their effects on the body. The first, cortisol, is related to capturing attention through heightening stress responses or curiosity. This effect is often experienced when engaging with the archetypal story of hero versus villain, where the former has an ultimate objective in mind but encounters obstacles along the way. The hero's role is to overcome these trials, typically despite setbacks, while also battling the villain throughout their journey. Because of situations the hero faces, stress responses or curiosity concerning what might happen are heightened, capturing the reader, listener, or observer's attention. There are many examples of this in film and literature, including Sigourney Weaver's feats as Ellen Ripley in Aliens and the main character's exploits in the Harry Potter series.

The most common response is to side with the protagonist, with a desire to see them meet their objective, overcome adversities, and best the villain. Consequently, this causes the body to start releasing the second of the two hormones, oxytocin. This hormone is found whenever humans feel close, or there is even a perception of closeness. The combination of these two hormones quickly engenders feelings of engagement and connection.

When clients share their collage stories, heroes and villains are not present in the traditional sense. Instead, these opposing characters emerge in their collage as experiences of internal conflict such as:

* ideas of right versus wrong or good versus bad
* past versus present or present versus future

DOI: 10.4324/9781003017028-12

- fear versus faith
- acceptance of self, versus judgement and guilt
- confidence versus imposter syndrome, low self-esteem, and so forth

These personal battles hold the coach's attention as they aspire to see the client overcome adversities, such as limiting beliefs. The same neural responses described in fictional stories occur here, as the hormones cortisol and oxytocin are released, creating engagement and connection that flows between teller and listener. Importantly, when people feel connected, they trust that they are in a safe space to express themselves freely and share personal feelings, insights, thoughts, and ideas (Plouffe, 2017). This open and honest dialogue is a prerequisite to the quality of communication necessary between client and coach to enable the formers exploration, discovery, and breakthroughs.

Additionally, research by Wudarczyk et al. (2013) describes the possible role of oxytocin in relationship building through storytelling as:

- engendering trust
- facilitating positive communication behaviour
- reducing anxiety and stress
- enabling empathy
- attention, recognition, and appraisal of social cues
- co-operating
- detecting and recognising emotions

Another advocate of personal storytelling is Dr Uri Hasson (Hasson TED Talks, 2016). His research found that personal stories, unlike pure facts, caused both the speaker and the listener to exhibit neural response patterns in the high-order areas of the brain (frontal and parietal cortex). After further studies, he concluded this was caused not only by the speaker's words and sound but notably by the meaning they conveyed. This connection between how the speaker's and listener's brains responded was stronger where they shared common ground, plus there was also better communication. As a result of these findings, Dr Hasson recommends that to find common ground, improve communication, and foster new ideas, people should engage in dialogue where speaking and listening are both valued. Storytelling is ideally suited to facilitate this form of exchange.

Client as Personal Storyteller | Deepening Awareness of Self

Self-awareness, generally described as "The extent to which people are consciously aware of their interactions or relationships with others and off [sic] their internal state" (Sutton, 2016, p. 2), is strongly linked to emotional intelligence and psychological well-being. Reflective practice and insight are essential for self-awareness, and according to Grant et al. (2002), the capacity to assess and manage these is integral to goal-oriented behaviour. For this reason, there is a strong argument for clients to increase their self-awareness to improve the possibility of achieving their definition of success. Within a coaching context, storytelling can play an invaluable role in supporting clients on their self-awareness journey to understand themselves and others better. Introducing the Collage Coaching Technique™ (CCT) as a creative coaching tool enriches and dynamically brings clients' stories to life. Because equipped with their collage as a tangible object, the expression of their experience deepens significantly as images and words combine.

Personal storytelling with the CCT does not follow the traditional structure of a beginning, middle, and end. Therefore, describing a client's collage composition and whatever they share as a story may confuse those who define it strictly in traditional terms. To alleviate any concerns that they cannot perceive a story, the coach can introduce different types of language, such as narrative or a visual tool. Regardless of the terminology, through their collage, the client has a way to discuss experiences that have informed their perspectives, responses, emotions, future desires, and other pertinent topics that may arise. These may relate to a snapshot in time, cover an extended period or focus on one major issue. Whatever the client discusses, they are experiencing an in-depth conversation with the coach and critically engaging in the same dialogue with themselves.

Achieving this depth within a session is facilitated by collage as a projective technique,[1] allowing what is hidden in the unconscious to surface visually. By circumnavigating external influences, editing and fact-checking, their collage represents an honest, outer expression of their internal processing and the resulting sense of self. As an intensely personal creation, it contains symbolic images and visual metaphors that evoke rich and emotive language to share their story. This wealth of words removes jargon, pretence, and clichés that might otherwise act as a barrier, impeding honesty and openness, not only with the coach but concerning the client's situation and feelings (Watts, 2020). In removing cursory conversations and allowing authentic expression, the pace at which conscious awareness and meaningful shifts occur for clients accelerates.

Catalysts of Conversation | A Picture Speaks a Thousand Words

Storytelling through collage eases the struggle for clients in knowing where or how to start talking about themselves. The reason for this is threefold:

1   Through the initial creative stages, clients have begun the process of reflecting on their experiences, thoughts, and emotions. As a result of this internal dialogue, clients engage in meaning-making and introspection. Therefore, when the time comes to share with the coach, they start with a degree of insight and clarity.
2   As a visual representation, clients can now literally see aspects of themselves reflected in their collage. This format acts as a tangible reference from which to express themselves, question existing assumptions, and divulge previously hidden understanding. Without their collage as a visual anchor, clients can find it challenging to articulate what they wish to address.
3   Personal interpretation means only clients know what their images represent. With the choice to only reveal what is comfortable, this option ensures they feel empowered and safe to share.

Engaging with a Range of Emotions

The positive attributes of engaging with storytelling are apparent. However, the coach should be aware that imagery can quickly generate a range of profound emotional impacts. Once the collage is complete, through an invitation to share their story, clients have an opportunity to be heard. For some clients, this will be the first time anyone will have listened to them in a meaningful way. Aware of the potential for breakthroughs and progress towards their goals, they may feel excitement and eagerness to begin. "I found the session enlightening, enjoyable, inspirational and beautiful. I was fantastically relaxed." Conversely, they may be experiencing anxiety and apprehension concerning what they will be revealing. Other clients will be somewhere between these two emotional states or experience them concurrently. "To do this you have to make yourself vulnerable, and this is scary. It can be emotional and exhausting, but very powerful and empowering."

These conflicting feelings echo in the storytelling. For example, besides joy and inspiration, clients can feel a sense of overwhelm or regret, often within the same session. The coach's role is to manage client expectations by informing them of these potential reactions in advance of the session. While recognising that if it occurs, even with awareness, it can still prove unexpected and challenging for clients. Usually, this precedes a sense of release at expressing their feelings in a safe space.

As the listener, the same chemical processes that create an emotional connection, engendering greater understanding, empathy and reflection, also present potential risks for the coach. There will be occasions when the client's and coach's stories connect either through the telling or where images resonate. As a result, the coach may become too engaged or invested in the client's story and forget that it is theirs to own and shape. Intentionally maintaining boundaries without losing the capacity to engage and respond authentically to clients minimises this risk.

Sharing and Shaping Their Story

Research suggests that stories are used as a way of digesting and making sense of information (Mighall, 2013). Therefore, once clients begin sharing, their story is told without interruption, allowing it to unfold and take shape in their own time and words. In the context of coaching, storytelling as a form of meaning-making is enhanced through collage, as clients also share their reflections, analysis, and discoveries made during the creative process. As Branthwaite (2002, p. 169) states, "Language has to be consciously understood before it can be expressed." Therefore, in finding the words to articulate and frame these thought processes, clients consolidate and clarify their insights and learning. Consequently, they also feel better able to express this to others.

Client Reflections

"I usually struggle to understand how I feel and what I'm thinking, so then find it difficult to explain this to others. But through the images I was able to express my emotions. Because I was able to express them, I better understood them and importantly was able to explain to others how I felt in a way they could understand." (Lisa)

"I certainly believe the process of creating a collage allowed me to explore my own vision and then enable me to articulate it clearly to others in a way I have never been able to do before. I honestly believe it helped me get the job." (Kelli)

During the narrative, it is also common for information that was unknown to the client to surface as a-ha moments. Often accompanied by phrases such as, "I hadn't realised that until I started to talk about it." With insights arriving in this way, clients know these revelations result from internal processing and not from an external source. As they learn to trust these moments as intuitive knowledge, they become more confident using these a-ha moments as a personal resource, whether it surfaces through collaging or in other ways.

The Coaching Conversation

In valuing the client's unique voice, it is appropriate for the coach to remain completely attentive and focused on the storyteller and how they convey their story. Not just orally, by sound and intonation, but also visually through body language and facial expression. In listening and watching mindfully, it is noticeable that as they share, clients reiterate areas of most importance to them, reflected in the way they tell their story and the emphasis placed on particular images. Furthermore, clients will point to and touch images as they talk. How they do this can indicate the nature of their relationship with it and what it holds for them. The coach notices these movements on the client's behalf, such as repeated contact, tracing around, and closer inspection. If the client discusses the image(s) during the coaching conversation, this physiological information is available to share with them as appropriate. As embodied cognition, this knowledge can help them connect to an alternative source of insight by accessing the totality of what they expressed.

However, it is only in careful observation and listening that the coach will achieve this awareness level. Therefore, coaches are discouraged from taking notes at this stage of the process. While this approach may be unfamiliar territory for the coach and create a level of apprehension concerning remembering the content of the client conversation, the nature of initiating storytelling through collage means that nothing of the story is lost. Instead, it is captured in a visually tangible way and can be revisited at any stage. Through practice, coaches learn to trust the process, the client, and their intuition, at which point this approach becomes easier. Notwithstanding this recommendation, if it substantially increases confidence, the coach can ask the client's permission to take notes of what they assess to be words or phrases of consequence. The client may also wish to make notes later during the coaching conversation.

Developing the Story

Following the storytelling, the coach demonstrates an appreciation of the trust placed in them by thanking the client for sharing. In coaching, relating a story is always personal, but especially where it may contain painful or embarrassing content. The likelihood is that clients have shown vulnerability by exposing private information concerning unresolved and challenging memories, emotions, and mindsets. Therefore, while acknowledging the privilege of hearing deeply personal details about them, this small gesture also builds the coaching relationship. With the coaching conversation as the next stage, this act creates a natural bridge for the coach to join the story, enabling it to evolve, revealing insights and meaning through further exploration.

In transitioning from a free-flowing story to replying to the coach's questions and comments, some clients will attempt to respond in a way they believe to be correct. One reason for this is the fear of sounding foolish or 'wrong,' thinking that essentially there is a 'right' answer. This type of reaction is distinguishable from when clients intentionally take the time they need to consider and process before commenting. Staying attuned, particularly to clients' physiology, ensures the coach will recognise when they are overanalysing and filtering what they say, rather than contemplating and remaining authentic. In this instance, reminders that the space is safe and confidential, there is no correct answer or necessity to edit themselves, suffices as reassurance. Consequently, continued reflection and elicitation of their images' true meaning occur through the conversation that follows the flow of uncensored words.

The purpose here is to work alongside the client to facilitate more in-depth understanding, insight, and conscious awareness. Therefore, as well as ascertaining which images the client would like to discuss by asking directly, the coach is guided by points of emphasis and strong emotions evident in the original storytelling. In adopting this approach, the direction continues to be led by the client, thereby supporting learning and growth in the most important areas to them.

A proportion of the observation relates to details clients have not shared in an individual image or overall collage, including unnoticed elements connected to areas already discussed. Once remarked upon by the coach, clients are inclined to either state that they had not noticed or that it was not what drew them to the image and is therefore irrelevant. With the latter, acknowledge their perspective while adding that their unconscious mind noticed. The client can then decide whether to explore this new information.

Throughout the coaching conversation, expect symbols and visual metaphors to trigger associative trains of thought that contain subject matter not represented in the collage. Even a portion of the client's story will include complexity. As such, these associations peel back layers, revealing more of the client as they get closer to ascertaining the core message held in the original image. Equally, the association can diverge in unexpected directions with the same effect. Following the thread with the client and holding the space allows for this new understanding to emerge. In doing so, a single image can offer unimagined breadth and depth for meaningful shifts that support their personal development and the opportunity to create change.

Client Reflections

(See Figure 9.2.1)

During her storytelling, one of the first thoughts Trinity shared was as follows:

"Although I don't know what it will be, the fireworks represent that whatever I'm going to do in life is going to be big and have an impact. In the same way that fireworks are bright and loud. So, yeah, I was very much drawn to them and this woman who has fireworks coming out of her head and she's standing very tall and erect. I love that image too, or I should say I see it as a woman, it might not be, but for me that's female empowerment."

Because of the emphasis placed on the firework image, I revisited it with Trinity during the coaching conversation, which led to further insight.

"I really do love fireworks, they're a spectacular invention and so beautiful. You go out on a cold crisp night and everyone hovers around, even though it's chilly. I don't know, I just think there's something magical about them and the scale of them. They light up the sky. I take real joy from them, which I hadn't said before. I just mentioned the boldness representing what I will do in the future, because I have this feeling that whatever it is will have an impact. But I think it also means that whatever it is I will enjoy it. That's important, because that's what's missing from my current role and it's not just about being good at something, it's about enjoying it. It also ties in with what I shared earlier when I realised that what I most want in my future is to feel joy. So actually, it's not about just being joyous, but being that in whatever I do in my future career." (Trinity)

In reviewing the image, Trinity accessed embodied memories of firework displays, allowing her to unlock insightful information not initially expressed through the image. Consequently, in remembering her joy of fireworks, the deeper meaning of the image emerged along with its connection to previous knowledge gained through her collage.

This merging of metaphor with memories and embodied cognition, triggered by the visual nature of collage, is an invaluable source of knowledge made available to clients through in-depth storytelling.

Continuing the Conversation

Although the coaching conversation is integral to the clients' discovery, clarity, and decision making, it is not the culmination of their storytelling. A client may choose to share their story with a broader audience. There is an element of risk associated with this activity outside of the coaching relationship, explicitly concerning how someone may project and interpret the collage and its images according to their circumstances. To mitigate this occurrence clients are reminded that although other perspectives are valuable for reflection, they are not substitutes for trusting their own insight. Therefore, if another person suggests an alternative meaning, they should first examine whether it resonates with them before considering it for reflection. As the risk is manageable, continued storytelling should not be discouraged because:

- it serves to deepen connection and embodiment through repeated telling
- alternative perspectives increase awareness and understanding
- clients report a beneficial impact on their relationships with others

"Questions from others about the collage have enriched my understanding. They noticed important details that are deeply relevant, yet I hadn't noted." (Stefano)

Case Study

Sarah created a collage during a group workshop with the theme of creative leadership. Her role as an external consultant for the NHS involved working with a team to improve Children's Services. Unfortunately, she was finding this challenging. The metaphor she used to describe it was like being an uninvited guest in someone's messy home whose job was to bring order and efficiency in a place where they were not wanted, represented on her collage by an untidy room. In contrast, the inclusion of a tidy room positioned next to the disordered one, reflected the organisation and structure she sought to create. She spoke at length about this issue that left her feeling alienated and like an outsider, inviting other participants to consider that situation for themselves. Sarah knew the children, with their untold stories (depicted by empty picture frames), were the focus of changing the service. However, the dynamics between her and the team meant they sometimes lost sight of this purpose. As a consultant, she believed they thought her focus was financial and not the children, consequently straining their relationship and impacting their ability to work effectively and implement the changes.

Sarah decided to share her completed collage with the NHS team she was working with, believing it would help them understand her position and passion for the children whose lives they were all trying to improve. Two weeks later, she sent me an email saying she'd shared the collage with her client, their immediate team, as well as her boss. She described how it enabled others to share their interpretation of her collage and the elements that touched them. Sarah said it was a positive turning point in how she went forward with her client and was particularly pleased to understand how creative leadership could positively impact her work.

Never Ending Story

Personal storytelling through collage provides clients with the insight, knowledge, and confidence to speak from a place of authenticity recognised by the listener. The ability to communicate in this fashion originates from reflecting, evaluating, and meaning-making using the symbols and metaphors in their collage. Subsequently, self-awareness increases as clients articulate their experiences, thought processes, emotions, values, and other aspects of their lives. Equipped with this clarity of thought, it lies within their power to effect positive change through focused decision making. Moreover, like a ripple effect, in sharing their collage outside of the coaching session, the client extends their story's potential to influence beyond themselves.

Bibliography

Branthwaite, A. (2002). Investigating the power of imagery in marketing communication: Evidence-based techniques. *Qualitative Market Research: An International Journal, 5*(3), 164–171. https://doi.org/10.1108/13522750210432977

Grant, A. M., Franklin, J., & Langford, P. (2002). The self-reflection and insight scale: A new measure of private self-consciousness. *Social Behavior and Personality, 30*(8), 821–836. https://doi.org/10.2224/sbp.2002.30.8.821

Hasson TED Talks. (2016). *Uri Hasson: This is your brain on communication | TED Talk | TED.com.* www.ted.com/talks/uri_hasson_this_is_your_brain_on_communication

Mighall, R. (2013). *Only Connect: The Art of Corporate Storytelling.* LID publishing.

Plouffe, T. (2017). *To Build Connection on Your Team, Skip Icebreakers and Talk About Photography.* Harvard Business Review. https://hbr.org/2017/10/to-build-connection-on-your-team-skip-icebreakers-and-talk-about-photography

Smith, J. A. (2016). *The science of the story | Berkeley News.* Berkeley News. https://news.berkeley.edu/berkeley_blog/the-science-of-the-story/

Sutton, A. (2016). Measuring the effects of self-awareness: Construction of the self-awareness outcomes questionnaire. *Europe's Journal of Psychology, 12*(4), 645–658. https://doi.org/10.5964/ejop.v12i4.1178

Watts, A. (2020). *A rich visual language | The Psychologist.* The Psychologist. https://thepsychologist.bps.org.uk/rich-visual-language

Wudarczyk, O. A., Earp, B. D., Guastella, A., & Savulescu, J. (2013). Could intranasal oxytocin be used to enhance relationships? Research imperatives, clinical policy, and ethical considerations. In *Current Opinion in Psychiatry* (Vol. 26, Issue 5, pp. 474–484). https://doi.org/10.1097/YCO.0b013e3283642e10

PART 2 | STORYTELLING IN GROUPS

Group interactions are complex, affected by demographics, culture, individual circumstances, belief systems, personal agendas, and so on (Gray, 2019). This diversity influences interactions and can create barriers, which stifle communication, hinder the development of authentic relationships and effective collaboration, or equally enrich learning opportunities. With its capacity to foster connections and build relationships, storytelling provides a forum for group members to interact in an engaging, informal, and creative way that bridges differences to effect meaningful and sustainable change.

Benefits of Group Work

The theory and principles of using collage as a tool for storytelling in groups are the same as personal coaching. However, there are additional benefits:

- building relationships and group cohesion
- combining collective knowledge
- retaining information
- conflict resolution
- improving levels of engagement

Building Relationships and Group Cohesion | "I See Your Point"

Relationships are most comfortable when people see themselves reflected in others. In a group, these connections provide a sense of unity and cohesion between individuals, allowing them to be more open and tolerant where there are differences. As a result, they are more likely to achieve desired collective outcomes. However, in places where groups form from diverse individuals, such as organisations, the task of finding commonality takes more time and effort. In enabling engagement, connection, and honest and open dialogue, storytelling through collage is an accessible and creative tool to expedite this process.

Stories are to be told and heard. While someone speaks, others are compelled to listen, and vice versa. This interactive act of sharing and listening creates a relationship of interdependence between the group as they rely on each other for the process to work (Willox et al., 2010). This first step of engaging with other group members is made easier by sharing through images, as personal truths are expressed using symbols and metaphors. Each time other group members experience resonance due to similar visual interpretations, experiences, values and so on, a connection occurs between the teller and listeners as they recognise a part of themselves in another's story. Furthermore, within the group, there is also a sense of "You have trusted me by disclosing something of yourself; in exchange, I will share something of myself." When this occurs, relationships deepen, and trust increases as individuals reveal more of themselves as the stories develop. This shift is reflected by a change of energy in the room, often expressed physiologically, through the body language of leaning in, nodding, and eye contact.

Because listeners become more willing and able to relate to the story and teller, thinking also evolves as members move from a place where they protect and promote their ideas to one where they are more open and receptive to hearing the contributions of others (Plouffe, 2017). Typically, in this process of creating meaningful connections and valuing other's voices, the prospect of successful collaboration and creative problem-solving also accelerates. As a tool for fostering positive relationships and cohesion, even before discussion starts, the CCT lays the foundations for developing connections as individuals simultaneously engage in the same creative process of making their collage. As personal storytelling begins, cohesion is reinforced as similarities and resonance mean that multiple stories often merge into a single narrative (Lipson et al., 1999). This outcome occurs whether group members make individual collages or co-create one that draws multiple images and experiences into a single collaborative composition.

Case Study | Sharing the Same Story

A group of women attended one of my public workshops. The theme was Building Confidence and Clarity at a Crossroad. One of the women had been made redundant; a couple of them had either a child going to university or starting school for the first time, while another had recently become a divorcee. As they shared their individual stories, the others listened attentively, and it soon became apparent that there was a common thread. Despite their different circumstances, the story they told wove into that of a woman facing loss, feelings of uncertainty and anxiety. Yet, this woman remained hopeful and resolved to create a positive future. In the process of this collective story unfolding and evolving, each woman spoke of the courage and resilience she needed before drawing on each other's experiences and wisdom as they individually decided their next steps. Although the women had attended the workshop as strangers, they left agreeing to continue their journey together.

By interacting in this way, individuals quickly develop a sense of community and belonging. Because storytelling through collage effectively facilitates genuine group cohesion, it is an invaluable tool to establish connections at the beginning of a course or where time is limited.[2]

Combining Collective Knowledge

Personally constructed knowledge is not an absolute fact. However, according to Taylor & Ladkin (2009), within organisations, some managers believe their understanding of complex issues is the only objective truth. Unfortunately, dismissing other perspectives pervades society generally. In these instances, story is a powerful tool for developing a more open and accepting approach for those who exhibit inflexible attitudes to alternative viewpoints. Because, as Drumm (2013, p. 5) summarises, "Story has the ability to create and communicate many personal truths and not just one objective truth."

Skilfully facilitated group storytelling ensures the richness and diversity inherent in groups, with their contrasting opinions are heard, as opposed to a single representative or dominant voice. Furthermore, working with visual metaphors removes the hierarchy and barriers that language can create by moving away from the notion of right or wrong. This perspective recognises that all contributions are valid, including the exploration of the emotional alongside the cognitive. Therefore, the emphasis is on making comments that expand, enhance, inquire, debate, and add value rather than diminish or dismiss the story. Attributing meaning to the metaphors and story through reflecting, accepting, integrating, or querying new information creates a fertile environment for ongoing exploration and alternative ways of thinking to flourish. This approach ensures the collage and the knowledge it contains continue evolving and providing learning opportunities for individuals and the group. As a result, collaborative storytelling means individual group members' knowledge, experience, and values combine into a collective augmented resource that improves outcomes and decisions by being better balanced.

Retaining Information

As an experiential technique, storytelling means group members are involved with and responsible for their individual and collective learning and development. Because this learning is based on information gleaned from working with metaphors, it originates from a well of internal knowledge and resources. Therefore, retaining this new material is enhanced because there is a deep connection to the individual. At points of resonance with other group members, this retention extends to them, and as the connection increases, so does the ability to retain the information.[3] Moreover, because images are memorable, in recalling them, the story and meaning also re-emerge into conscious awareness. As a permanent, tangible record, the collage serves as a visual reminder that the group can use to reflect on their discussions, outcomes, and decisions.

Reaching Resolutions

During storytelling, the images and interpretations are just as likely to surface differences in values, mental models, and belief systems as create resonance and connection. These can highlight previously hidden assumptions and biases that exist at an individual and collective level. However, the images and metaphors provide a vehicle through which judgements can be discussed and questioned without direct reference to an individual or as a personal statement (Taylor & Ladkin, 2009). The effect of metaphorically stepping back and distancing means that the issue is more likely to be heard, rather than attributed to personality differences.

Consequently, through alternative interpretations of an image, differences are reframed as a source of curiosity and fact-finding instead of conflict or concern. From this perspective, subsequent explorative discussions serve to clarify an individual's understanding of a situation. Although this may still prove uncomfortable for some and not necessarily lead to a group agreement, a cycle of collective dialogue and reflection creates a space for more considered responses. In turn, this way of engaging with others can diffuse difficult situations and resolve differences in a non-confrontational manner. In terms of reaching resolutions in personal and professional relationships, this is undoubtedly beneficial.

Case Study

During a strategic planning workshop for a small business, the image of the baby elephant entering the water resonated with a team member. They described it as representing the new business service, while the adult was their established services and brand. They felt ready and able to move forward with this behind them, just as the adult gently nudged the infant forward into the water. They saw the light as symbolic of hope, possibility, and positivity. However, another colleague, Marcus, interpreted the adult elephant as pushing the baby off the security of the stones, into new and unknown territory. He felt the baby elephant was fearful and anxious. Marcus then explained how he was reticent to move forward with an ambitious strategic change of direction at this time. His colleagues were surprised at this revelation, believing they were all on board with moving forward at pace, having not seen it as a major change.

Figure 10.2.1 Photograph by Comfreak from Pixabay.

As the conversation developed, the image remained a reference source as they explored how the symbolism of light influenced their perceptions. Marcus had seen the light as shining a spotlight on vulnerability rather than illuminating the way ahead. He described a personal experience where a new product taken to market had failed at a high financial and emotional cost to himself. Consequently, he was extremely cautious about trying something similar again.

With this new information, the team's discussion focused on how to resolve the issue. As part of this process, the group used other images to clarify expectations around the business development. By the end of the workshop, they reached a consensus about implementing the strategy, including the pace of change and support they could offer to Marcus.

Improving Levels of Engagement

There are usually differences in individuals' willingness to engage in facilitated group work and discussions. Fortunately, the format of using a collage to generate dialogue coupled with the focus on valuing all voices and contributions minimises the possibility of dominant voices while enabling full participation by all group members.

For example, if someone is experiencing low confidence, they may initially feel reluctant to share their story with the rest of the group. However, the collage improves the likelihood of involvement because:

- once others commence sharing, neurochemicals are released, which facilitate the sense of connection, trust, and belonging[4]
- as a projective technique, the client can choose to speak about the images in the third person and thereby avoid specific personal references

- the images act as a catalyst for dialogue, so negate apprehension concerning how to proceed with the narrative
- participation in the 'gathering' and 'creating' stages before invited to share engenders mindfulness which lowers anxiety[5]
- the collage rather than the speaker becomes the focus of attention
- although rare, if necessary, clients can opt to literally speak from behind the collage, holding it up, so it acts like a shield[6]

Furthermore, larger groups of eight or more can be broken down into smaller conversation units, reducing potential feelings of anxiety and empowering everyone to contribute. The value of this lies in the opportunity to hear viewpoints that may otherwise remain silent. Only in hearing every voice do possibilities arise for greater awareness, a better understanding of others, and the development and pooling of collective knowledge. For this reason, before the end, time is dedicated to a joint review and reflection on the experience. Concluding in this way consolidates discovery and learning while reminding clients to value every voice and story, including their own.

Success Through Storytelling

Coaching with collage is a powerful tool for facilitating storytelling that creates opportunities for open, honest, and non-judgemental dialogue when working with the diversity inherent in groups. Therefore, it is particularly beneficial when dealing with the complexities of change at a group level, such as in organisations. Significantly, as visual references, the symbols and metaphors play a role in enriching each person's language while also providing clarity. As a result, values, mental models, biases, and emotions influencing perspectives and behaviour surface. Now they are available for group discussion, questioning, learning, reaching resolutions, and successful collaboration. The breadth and value in these outcomes ensure the CCT is applicable anywhere that requires better conversations.

Notes

1 See Chapter 9 | Part 2: The Creative Process as an Expression of 'Self'
2 Collage Coaching cards are as effective in creating connections and particularly useful where time is limited (See resources in Chapter 15).
3 See Chapter 6 | The Power of Visual Communication.
4 See Chapter 10 | Part 1: Individual Storytelling.
5 See Chapter 9 | Part 2: The Creative Process as an Expression of 'Self'.
6 I have only experienced it once while facilitating a group workshop in a therapeutic setting alongside a therapist.

Bibliography

Drumm, M. (2013). *The role of personal storytelling in practice | Iriss.* www.iriss.org.uk
Gray, R. P. (2019). *Art Therapy and Psychology.* Routledge.
Lipson, R., Craig, L., & Mealman, A. (1999). *Collaborative Ways of Knowing: Storytelling, Metaphor and the Emergence of the Collaborative Self.* http://citeseerx.ist.psu.edu/viewdoc/download?doi= 10.1.1.526.1074&rep=rep1&type=pdf

Plouffe, T. (2017). *To Build Connection on Your Team, Skip Icebreakers and Talk About Photography.* Harvard Business Review. https://hbr.org/2017/10/to-build-connection-on-your-team-skip-icebreakers-and-talk-about-photography

Taylor, S. S., & Ladkin, D. (2009). Understanding arts-based methods in managerial development. *Academy of Management Learning and Education, 8*(1), 55–69. https://doi.org/10.5465/AMLE.2009.37012179

Willox, A. C., Harper, S. L., Bridger, D., Morton, S., Orbach, A., & Sarapura, S. (2010). Co-Creating Metaphor in the Classroom for Deeper Learning: Graduate Student Reflections. *International Journal of Teaching and Learning in Higher Education, 22*(1), 71–79. https://eric.ed.gov/?id=EJ913531

Putting it into Practice

11 Facilitating a Safe Space for Coaching with a Creative Technique

In the context of working with people in coaching or therapy, a safe space is one where clients do not feel threatened or at risk from emotional harm, such as embarrassment, shame, fear, guilt, or failure. Instead, it is a place of trust and mutual respect that enables clients to express themselves openly and honestly. Here they can explore, confront, and allow themselves to be confronted by things that concern and challenge them. While also acknowledging and celebrating where they have demonstrated courage, wisdom, creativity, vulnerability, tenacity, and other qualities that enable them to excel and flourish.

This space includes a physical environment that supports the psychological sense of safety. It is described as safe because when clients are there, they can create and be heard without reservation or fear of judgement. Furthermore, there is no right or wrong, good or bad, so clients are more at ease and open to taking risks. Coach and client are equal partners as they co-create together, and there is full acceptance of the client exactly as and where they are in life, allowing them to present their whole self. Essentially, the space created facilitates exploration and breakthroughs they can build on. The coach's responsibility is to foster this safe environment enabling clients to get the best out of engaging with a creative coaching technique.

Courage to Be Creative

Using an arts-based method (ABM) for coaching and working with the unconscious brings additional considerations when creating a safe space. Although clients have chosen to use the Collage Coaching Technique™ (CCT), there may still be a degree of apprehension of what the creative process may require of them. Particularly potential anxieties around their artistic or creative abilities and concerns over what may surface from their unconscious. It takes courage to question what is known, see things differently and be open to what may emerge in a visually tangible way. Significantly, clients are literally committing a part of themselves to paper, not forgetting that it is likely to include deeply personal thoughts, feelings and potentially entrenched mental models and beliefs not yet consciously known. As a tangible, and at least in that moment, permanent construct, there is a risk that others will infer meaning and make judgements from their creation. This can be a daunting and vulnerable position to put themselves in as they entrust the coach with an innermost part of themselves, embodied in the physical action of presenting their collage. Therefore, it is imperative to create and hold that safe space as a metaphorical container for clients. Fortunately, coaches can alleviate any apprehension and anxiety by implementing the following guidelines for all clients, regardless of whether they have voiced uncertainties.

DOI: 10.4324/9781003017028-14

When Not to Use the Collage Coaching Technique™

The coaching contract will acknowledge that coaching does not involve diagnosing or treating psychological disorders or traumas. Therefore, because working with the unconscious poses risks around what may surface, it is recommended that only practitioners such as counsellors, therapists, mental health specialists, or coaches with the necessary training work with clients in the following circumstances:

*   after a recent bereavement (a minimum of eight months afterwards)[1]
*   if the client is aware they have unresolved traumas
*   when a person has a clinical diagnosis of severe mental health issues

Each coach will need to assess their capabilities and skillset. Where the coach does not feel sufficiently equipped to work with these clients, they must advise them that, for their emotional safety, they cannot work with them. Outside of these instances, if a problem arises during the coaching session, clients are given space and time to manage their feelings. If necessary, with their permission, they can be referred to a GP, other suitable professional or relevant support. In the unlikely eventuality that it is a safeguarding issue (risk to themselves or others), permission to make a referral is not required. Because of the reason clients seek coaching, reinforced by the contract, these outcomes are unlikely. However, best practice dictates that care is taken when working with the unconscious, and guidelines are followed. These initial steps of stating clearly who the CCT is unsuitable for and always working to a theme lay the foundation for the safe space, substantially limiting the risk of negative experiences for both client and coach.

The Need for a Theme

All individual coaching sessions and facilitated group workshops must have a clearly defined theme.[2] This theme, agreed in advance with the client, is another container, creating parameters around their unconscious thoughts. Although the client does not concentrate on it as they work through the creative process, it serves as a primer[3] by preparing the unconscious mind to retrieve information related to the subject. Because, without focus, surfacing meaningful insights to support personal development decreases. Additionally, the mind is free to wander where it will, with results that could be detrimental for the client and potentially the coach. When working with images to access unconscious thinking, there is also a risk that one may act as a key that unexpectedly opens the door to something the unconscious has locked away. Often, these are subjects and experiences that people find too difficult to deal with or are ashamed to confront or resolve. Therefore, although what comes out is usually beneficial, it cannot be guaranteed. Nevertheless, the likelihood is that even extremely difficult material that emerges links to the theme. Therefore if the client is willing, it can be explored during their coaching.

The Physical Environment

Akin to art therapy rooms, the space in which coaching with collage or other ABMs occur must be, and feel, like a secure environment. Because what may surface can be uncomfortable and challenging, the purpose of the space is to foster trust and enable reflection in a peaceful and calm atmosphere. Therefore, preferably it will feel welcoming, be free from clutter, contain plant life, and provide natural light. The layout needs to be conducive to using art materials and facilitating a visually creative activity, with a suitably sized table, comfortable chairs and high-quality materials that are fit for purpose. In providing this space and resources, the coach inspires the client's confidence and trust by demonstrating they understand the best conditions required to coach creatively with an arts-based technique.

Complete privacy during coaching is imperative to ensure the client does not feel exposed or intimidated and will not be interrupted or distracted. Whilst coaches are aware of this, because it is an arts-based activity, the client, whether an individual or organisation, may not be. For example, a business once offered me a room with glass walls and doors positioned centrally in an open-plan office. Participants would have been in full view of their colleagues and vice versa. However, the client had not seen this as problematic until I raised concerns during planning, at which stage they found a suitable alternative. Because the physical space has a significant impact on the creative process, coaches should acquire as much detail about the room in advance to avoid turning up to an unsuitable venue.

Like those artists, with the luxury of owning a studio, who craft the ideal environment to foster inspiration and the flow of creative energy, coaches can endeavour to replicate this type of space for their clients.

Practitioner Preparation

The practitioner is the single most critical influence in ensuring the space feels safe for clients. Therefore, when preparing the environment, it is essential that the coach also implements practices to prepare themselves: psychologically, emotionally, physically, and for some people, spiritually. These practices relate to both longer-term professional development and actions undertaken immediately before the session.

In advance of a coaching session, my preference is to set aside time for a mindful mediation exercise and be still in the space where I will work with my client. The intention is to make sure I remain fully present during the coaching by setting aside personal concerns and challenges. Regular mindfulness practice also heightens awareness concerning remaining open, curious, and non-judgemental. This skill is essential when coaching and particularly significant when working with imagery. In this context, the ability to recognise when the client's images resonate prevents projection and the instinctive reaction of responding subjectively or commenting on the collage's aesthetics. Furthermore, as mindfulness focuses on paying attention, on purpose, to the present moment, habitual use develops 'noticing'[4] as a transferable skill for application during the coaching conversation.

When integrating the CCT as a coaching tool, best practice for coaches is to create collages at regular intervals using the technique. Only in undertaking this as part of continued professional and personal development can they gain a thorough appreciation of the client experience. As a result of this coaches can offer their clients authentic insight into the process. Additionally, the approach delivers the same beneficial outcomes for coaches as clients, empowering exploration of the unconscious mind to increase self-awareness, a core coaching skill.

In both the short and long-term, whatever measures coaches take to prepare themselves for a creative coaching session, the purpose is to develop and train the mind and emotions to remain focused on the client. As energy and attention stay centred there, it establishes rapport, fostering a sense of trust and safety. Consequently, space emerges where clients feel comfortable and confident to co-create and engage in deeper personal exploration and discovery.

Music

Music can have a psychological and physiological influence at an individual and group level, regulating mood and fostering a specific emotional state (Fernández-Sotos et al., 2016; Heshmat, 2019). Soothing, relaxing music is chosen for use during the CCT because various research shows that it slows the heart rate, engendering a state of calm and well-being (Levitin & Hamilton, 2016). Induced by a melody and rhythm that reinforce feelings of emotional safety, clients are less likely to experience irritability or anxiety in this state of calm and relaxation, as evidenced by the following feedback.

"I'm so glad there was music in the background because in silence, you can more easily hear the whirring in your head. When I started to become distracted, I could tune into the music instead, which carried me back to the calming atmosphere where I could stay present and focused. Music fills those gaps where the whirring would have been." (Patricia).

In recognition that music experience and interpretation are subjective, clients are informed of the purpose of incorporating music, with choices around whether to play it and the option to discontinue. Besides the neurological benefits, music is instrumental in creating a safe space for clients who are uncomfortable with silence. Ambient music fills the silence as clients gather their images and make the collage. Anecdotally, these clients report feeling less self-conscious and more at ease.

Because of the benefits that enhance the client's experience, playing music[5] during the CCT is highly recommended. To ensure clients have their coach's undivided attention, playing music does not occur while the collage is shared or during the coaching conversation.

Mindfulness

Mindfulness is an effective meditative exercise to prepare clients for coaching with collage by shifting awareness into the present moment, meaning clients are fully engaged in the process without immediate concerns for the past or future. Whenever possible, the coaching session begins with a five to ten-minute body scan. The exercise not only serves as a form of relaxation it also acts as an anchor, as the coach can guide clients back to their breath during their consultation if necessary. This strategy is beneficial if they experience any of the following:

- start to feel stuck
- prematurely move into more cognitive ways of thinking
- experience heightened emotional periods
- begin to feel anxious

Returning to mindful breathing restores clients to a sense of ease and safety with the process, the coach, and themselves.

However, only coaches with the knowledge, skills, and confidence to guide their clients through a mindfulness exercise should do so. For others, there are alternatives, for example, sharing pre-recorded versions.[6] Alternatively, the coach may choose to omit this preparatory exercise because, as an ABM, the CCT naturally engenders a state of mindfulness as clients gather images and compose their collage (Baqaeen, 2018).

While a mindfulness exercise is not obligatory, it adds value to the client's creative coaching experience, promoting a sense of well-being and safety. Therefore, the advice is to incorporate it whenever practicably possible.[7]

Client Reflections

"I've not been very successful the couple of times I've done mindfulness before. But here in this space, I was fully immersed in it, and that was really good. So that when I came out of it, my head was much clearer than it has been in a long time, and I could gather the way you should as I'd let go of what I'd come in the room to try and show; so that was positive I thought." (Trinity)

Group Work

Creating a Safe Space with Groups

Approaches for creating a psychological and physically safe space with groups are the same as working with an individual. However, there are further considerations, including group size and dynamics, potentially less influence over the physical environment, and the possibility of unwilling participants. Additionally, more people mean the number with concerns around creative expression, accessing the unconscious and allowing vulnerability potentially increases. In groups, these feelings may be exacerbated by an individual's sense of exposure because more people can witness their concerns. Consequently, maintaining a safe space in groups requires facilitation, as well as coaching skills.

Group Contracting

A group agreement or collective intentions, is essentially a contract that defines how members work together in a creative, productive, and respectful way that facilitates a sense of safety. Following best practice requires agreeing it between all group members, including the coach, at the start of the workshop. Depending on the setting, the contract may be written or remain a verbal agreement. Either way, it determines how individuals will conduct themselves within the group, focusing on behaviours that allow everyone to contribute meaningfully to discussions, ask questions, express differing opinions, and explore challenging issues. At a minimum, the contract includes confidentiality and respecting the group's diversity, regardless of individual beliefs or values. When working with the CCT, it should also incorporate the following:

- there are no right or wrong interpretations of images or a completed collage, therefore whether giving or receiving, an individuals' explanation is understood to be an opinion and not a fact
- personal expressions of emotion are an expected and accepted part of the process
- time is allowed to share the stories, and only the coach is responsible for managing time and drawing a story to a close
- if an individual chooses not to share details in their collage, this is accepted and respected

•   judgements are not passed on the collages' aesthetics

The contract also manages expectations because, with parameters of behaviour established, clients feel at ease in the group knowing actions outside of what was agreed are deemed unacceptable. This knowledge empowers and authorises them, individually and collectively, to safeguard the space for all members.

Managing Emotional Responses

The immediacy of images' emotional and psychological effects on individuals[8] does not change because people are working in a group. The distinction arises if someone becomes upset, is moved to tears or gets overwhelmed. On such occasions, the coach must consider the impact on other group members in conjunction with the individual. The introduction refers to the possibility of this occurrence, making it clear that emotional and physiological reactions to images are normal human responses, which can be embraced rather than seen as an impediment. Therefore, if such emotions surface, they reflect the client's strong sense of safety and trust by permitting themselves expression in tears as well as words.

After the introduction, if a group member discloses a recent bereavement or unresolved trauma, they are guided to approach the exercise like a vision board.[9] This technique involves choosing images around the theme rather than accessing the unconscious to gather them. Therefore, minimising the potential for tears caused by profoundly complex emotional or psychological issues surfacing.

Another way to ensure clients' emotional needs are supported is to facilitate groups with another coach. This approach allows the provision of individual attention as necessary.

Cultivating Certainty

Uncertainty can cause anxiety through the experience of lack of control. While coaching creatively cannot provide absolutes, aspects of the process are clearly defined, and here the coach can offer clients certainty to increase their comfort levels and reduce apprehension. With the CCT, reassurance comes by providing an overview of the three stages, ensuring everyone knows what to expect and when. Once the process starts, clients are guided step by step through each stage to prevent information overwhelm and allow them time to pause and reflect between each phase. During these transition points, the coach has an opportunity to check individuals' or the group's progress. Intentionally, this approach also maintains clients' focus on the present moment, removing potential concerns about remembering the next set of instructions.

Each stage of the CCT relies on specific group behaviours to maintain the safe space and engagement in the process. For example, any feelings of vulnerability are most likely to occur when personal storytelling through their collage; therefore, it is imperative to create a strong sense of safety at this point. Consequently, guidance given beforehand incorporates confidentiality, listening respectfully and offering and receiving alternative perspectives without judgement. Reminding the group of these already agreed behaviours lowers the risk of an individual dominating the conversation or anyone interrupting the storytelling, which may otherwise leave the teller feeling unheard and undervalued. Although the group size determines how storytelling is facilitated,[10] everyone has the opportunity to share their narrative with at least one other person. Besides consolidating learning and meaning-making, this creates connections and builds relationships, reinforcing the sense of safety that precedes a willingness to contribute openly and honestly.[11]

Final Thoughts

The intention of creating a safe space is not about clients never feeling uncomfortable, stretched, or challenged. These are a necessary part of exploration, discovery, and ultimately personal and professional growth. Instead, the safe space is intended to build trust and allow vulnerability by creating the psychological and physical environment that fosters this outcome. Involving both practical steps and particular skills, creating a safe space requires purposeful and intentional action on the part of the coach.

Notes

1 This time frame is based on my work with the bereavement group and advice given by the facilitators with in-depth experience in this field. After this period, discussion with the client should determine whether the CCT is suitable for them. If in any doubt, do not proceed.
2 Theme is used and not topic because, when writing a story, the latter refers to the "what" and focuses on facts and details. The theme pertains to the "why," the bigger picture that connects readers and reveals why the story matters. This definition reflects the nature of collage as a visual narrative and how the client's story is told.
3 See Chapter 7 | Coaching with the Unconscious.
4 See Chapter 8 | Part 2: Clean Language and the Coaching Conversation.
5 A music playlist is available to use for free on the resources page at unglueyou.co.uk. As creative commons work, under the licence agreement when coaching at a public venue the composer, Scott Buckley (www.scottbuckley.com.au) should be attributed.
6 A pre-recorded mindfulness meditation is available to use for free on the resources page at unglueyou.co.uk.
7 The time allocated by organisations for group work is not usually enough to incorporate a mindfulness exercise.
8 See Chapter 6 | The Power of Visual Communication.
9 See Chapter 4 | Beyond the Vision Board.
10 In workshops of 2–2.5 hours, six or less participants can share their collage as one group. With larger numbers participants should break into smaller discussion groups. If possible, the group gather at the end to reflect.
11 See Chapter 10 | Part 2: Storytelling in Groups.

Bibliography

Baqaeen, L. (2018). *Mindfulness in the art-making for employee well-being: An exploratory study on collage.* City, University of London.

Fernández-Sotos, A., Fernández-Caballero, A., & Latorre, J. M. (2016). Influence of tempo and rhythmic unit in musical emotion regulation. *Frontiers in Computational Neuroscience, 10*(AUG), 80. https://doi.org/10.3389/fncom.2016.00080

Heshmat, S. (2019). *Music, Emotion, and Well-Being | Psychology Today.* www.psychologytoday.com/us/blog/science-choice/201908/music-emotion-and-well-being

Levitin, D., & Hamilton, A. (2016). *Speaking of Psychology: Music and your health.* www.apa.org/research/action/speaking-of-psychology/music-health.aspx

12 Holding the Silence in Coaching

In the context of coaching with collage, the term 'hold the silence' represents a metaphorical container where the silence refers to a psychologically safe space that allows for reflection and contemplation. A crucial part of the coach's role is to hold this silence and create an environment where thoughts can become words, and there is no expectation of sound for its own sake. Instead, there is an acceptance that words may not be forthcoming for some time, but eventually, the client will fill the silence in a manner of their choosing. They must be allowed the opportunity to do this.

Unfortunately, many people dislike silence because it is unfamiliar, with the phrase 'awkward silence' encapsulating the expectation for constant dialogue. The uncomfortable nature of these silences is usually associated with feelings of anxiety, as people think they ought to be speaking but are unsure of what to say next. Consequently, in a bid to move things forward and ease feelings of discomfort and self-consciousness for both or either party, there may be a temptation for the coach to fill the container. Typically, by rephrasing the question, asking another one, or suggesting an answer. This response may be intuitive, but it is counterproductive to protecting the time to stop and think, which is the purpose of silence as a container.

Silence Is Golden

When working with the Collage Coaching Technique™ (CCT), silence occurs at the following stages:

* while the client is gathering images
* as the client creates their collage
* during the coaching conversation

The design of the first two stages includes engendering a state of mindfulness and flow[1] through working silently; therefore, there is no expectation for speech. However, during the coaching conversation, a client may be silent after an invitation to respond to a question or observation. If a choice is made by the coach, even unconsciously, to fill rather than hold this silence, there is a risk of adversely impacting the client's discovery when an insight may have been a breath away. Potentially, having a visual reference heightens the risk of overhasty involvement as the coach may project their interpretation unto the image. Therefore, mindfulness practice is highly recommended to minimise this risk while developing professional confidence and ease with this approach. Because when there is

DOI: 10.4324/9781003017028-15

comfort with the stillness and quiet, clients notice this and subsequently feel increased relaxation.

Preparing Clients for Silence

Before starting the coaching conversation, explaining that there is an expectation for extended periods of silence during this stage ensures clients are aware of and value the stillness that allows for personal discovery. Useful phrases to use before and during questions include:

1 You may find this challenging if you have not considered or thought about this before. So, take the time you need to gather your thoughts.
2 Take a moment to breathe deeply if you need to.
  • If the session started with a mindfulness exercise, the client could be guided back to their breath.
3 You do not have to try and find the right words or censor your response. There is no wrong answer.
4 Moments of silence are to be expected.
5 If the answer does not come now, be reassured that understanding is likely to surface later as you continue to reflect on your collage.

These phrases are also helpful when clients initially respond with, "I don't know." On some level they do, but may not want to answer for any or a combination of the following reasons:

• not trusting their intuition
• avoidance of, or seeking to end the silence
• they have never considered the question
• fear concerning discussing a subject that is painful or overwhelming
• embarrassment or shame
• difficulty articulating their response
• they need more time to process

Therefore, a considered response by the coach can provide reassurance while acknowledging the client's position and enabling time for reflection and insight.

Working with Silence in Groups

Group sessions using the CCT are decidedly different from working with individuals, especially when some participants are not there through choice, such as organisational programmes. Additionally, the group probably consists of people with alternative perspectives, experiences, and attitudes to working with an arts-based method (ABM). Such diversity impacts group dynamics and their willingness or ability to engage with the process and work in silence.[2]

The silence occurs at the same stages as with individual coaching sessions. At these times, there may be members of the group who find it challenging not to talk. Before each step, to minimise the chances of this occurring, the group are reminded that the purpose of working in silence is to prevent cognition over-riding unconscious thoughts, a consequence of engaging in conversation. By informing them in advance, if someone starts talking, the coach can refer to this guidance.

Unlike individual coaching, there is no co-creating[3] alongside the group. Instead, the coach acts as a facilitator, remaining mindfully observant of everyone in the room. This role means being comfortable maintaining silence as participants work through stages one and two, intervening only as necessary to support the creative process. To begin with, like holding the silence during the coaching conversation, this may feel awkward, coupled with thoughts of, "I should be 'doing' something." However, the fact is that being still is 'doing something,' as when coaching a group using the CCT, creating a space where all participants can work without interruption is essential. In the absence of this type of environment, connecting with the unconscious mind and entering a state of mindfulness and flow is more challenging.

Best practice requires coaches inexperienced at facilitation to develop the necessary skills and confidence using the CCT with individuals before undertaking group work.

Holding as Letting Go

The act of working alongside individuals in their personal growth also requires stepping aside to enable them to find their own way. Therefore, they should be allowed to set the pace at which things move on during dialogue. Whatever their answer or response looks like, it will come while the coach sits quietly at ease and gently breathes. This act of holding the silence requires patience and the knowledge that coaches are not in the business of fixing anyone and, therefore, do not have to rush the process. Not forgetting that for many clients, working creatively with an ABM in coaching is a rare and genuine opportunity to slow down and reflect effectively.

Notes

1 See Chapter 9 | Part 2: The Creative Process as an Expression of 'Self' (Flow, mindfulness and Art-Making).
2 Clients are guided to work without talking during specific parts of the process, but do not work in complete silence as background music is available.
3 See Chapter 9 | Part 3: Creativity in Practice (Co-creating with Clients).

13 Preparing a Group to Work with an Arts-Based Method

As an arts-based method (ABM), the Collage Coaching Technique™ (CCT) is a creative approach to working with groups. It offers an engaging and visual way for individual and collective elicitation and exploration of thoughts, gaining clarity, sharing information, and creating connections.

However, while the idea of using such a methodology for learning and development will appeal to some, to others, it is anathema, potentially in the realm of role-play!

Encouraging Engagement

Working with an ABM in group coaching invariably presents challenges. One reason for this is that participants will invariably hold one, or a combination, of the following different perspectives:

- concern
- curiosity
- cynicism
- keenness

Such diverse perceptions, and therefore expectations can create issues, especially if the group intends to create a single collage collaboratively. Fortunately, the introduction to the workshop can instill confidence and ensure everyone is comfortable and confident in engaging with an ABM.

Guidance for Introducing the Workshop

For the Concerned

Those who are concerned about participating in ABM workshops tend to use phrases such as "I'm no good at art," "I'm not creative" and "I can't draw." These individuals benefit from the reassurance that it is not about the level of their artistic skills or perceived creativity. Instead, the emphasis is on moving away from verbal centred language by using the art materials as a visual communication tool; consequently, they cannot do it wrong.

Additionally, it is helpful to acknowledge that school art classes were a time of anxiety and disappointment for many because their artwork was judged and graded based on its appearance. Unfortunately, this way of engaging with art remains the norm for many

DOI: 10.4324/9781003017028-16

people. However, accentuating that their collage will not be judged in any way considerably diminishes anxiety relating to the aesthetics.

With a reframe of the CCT away from a focus on art, alongside knowing their collage composition is not for visual appraisal, clients' confidence to express themselves through the materials increases. Those who felt concerned are now free to create without reservation, rather than leaving it to the 'creatives' in the room, reducing the occurrence of people becoming disengaged.

For the Curious

The curious are those who approach an ABM with a willingness to 'give it a go.' For these people, the focus is on inspiring them to play by engaging with the materials in a child-like manner. Accordingly, they are encouraged to trust the process, take risks with the materials, suspend preconceived ideas of what they will create, and remain open to possibilities.

However, because adults are not expected or encouraged to play, even the curious may experience reticence once faced with art materials. Should this occur, there is a reminder that the process is not related to artistic ability, nor is it a competition. Instead, the focus is on appreciating everyone's contribution as valid and adding value. In stating this categorically, the confidence to play will be a natural outcome of the creative process. Subsequently, curious individuals remain enthusiastic and bring that energy to the group, rather than feeling inhibited and cautious, believing they lack the required skillset.

For the Cynical

A person who shows cynicism regarding using an ABM will question its validity as a coaching or learning and development tool. They may perceive the approach as childish and pointless. Openly mentioning this viewpoint while acknowledging that perspectives and judgements originate from personal preferences, belief systems, values, and experiences, demonstrates an understanding of their position, reducing the risk of resistance.

While clarifying that it is child-like, not childish, those who approach the activity with scepticism are encouraged to adopt a child's qualities in terms of remaining open, curious, and non-judgemental. Working with the unconscious and intuition may also mean stretching their comfort zone. Therefore, to minimise potential withdrawal, the emphasis is on the CCT as a structured framework that includes analysis, editing, and assessment.

By acknowledging and understanding their perspective, the probability of positive engagement increases as their position shifts, and they remain open to possibilities. Otherwise, their doubt might find expression through comments or behaviours that undermine the validity of the process and impact the group dynamics.

For the Keen

Generally defining themselves as creative, the 'keen' come excited, eager, and usually with art experience in their personal or professional life. Nonetheless, their enthusiasm for participation in an ABM creates a different set of considerations. Because these individuals approach the workshop with positive expectations, they are more readily disappointed if their preconceived ideas are unmet. Additionally, there is the possibility that others may feel less competent working alongside someone confident in engaging with artistic processes.

For those who are keen, understanding the CCT as an opportunity for visual and creative expression deepens confidence in their ability to make a positive contribution to the group. While this benefits the individual and group, the emphasis remains on the creative process as a tool for accessing unconscious thinking and enabling cognitive awareness. By focusing attention here, rather than on individual artistic expression and skills, they are reminded of the purpose of applying an ABM in a learning and development context. Emphasising this stance also reinforces that everyone can make a meaningful contribution, not just those considered visually artistic. This approach manages expectations and minimises potential feelings of deflation or frustration without curbing their enthusiasm, joy, and anticipation of the collage-making process.

For the Coach

Everyone's art experience is different; recognising and accepting this is key to the successful facilitation of an ABM coaching workshop. Therefore, to ensure all positions are acknowledged, the workshop's introduction should weave in each of the four perspectives clients may hold. In drawing attention to potential concerns and resolutions from the outset, the coach can refer to them whenever necessary throughout the process. Preparing the group in this manner creates an environment where everyone can participate in their unique way, ensuring successful engagement with the CCT or other ABM.[1] Consequently, the individual and group experience the enrichment and added value that results from diverse contributions, perspectives, knowledge, and ideas.

Note

1 While written specifically for the CCT, the four perspectives are doubtless present whenever working with groups using an ABM. The majority of the solutions offered to support each perspective are transferable to other arts-based methodologies.

14 Coaching with Collage Online

An attribute of coaching with collage is the tactile nature of the materials, essentially magazines, scissors, and glue. Often there is learning from how clients engage with these resources. Understandably, therefore, the idea of using the Collage Coaching Technique™ (CCT) online, with digital images may seem counter-intuitive, at least initially. However, the coronavirus pandemic, that had a global impact in 2020 and beyond, highlighted the necessity to adapt and, where possible, offer online alternatives to continue supporting coaching clients. In creating an online version, it became apparent that as the process and outcomes are the same, nothing is lost compared to the classic[1] CCT approach (Watts, 2020). Instead, there is merely a difference in how clients interact with the resources. Furthermore, a digital option allows those clients who would otherwise be unable to access it due to their location or lack of magazines, to benefit from coaching with collage. As with the offline version, coaches are encouraged to attend training prior to using this tool with their clients.

Coaching Creatively Online | Facilitating Engagement

While an online version of the CCT increases accessibility, akin to the offline version, there are considerations in terms of client engagement and the barriers they may face; primarily, recognising that individuals have different comfort levels and experience with technology. For some clients, the digital approach may prove easier to engage with, particularly to those who consider the physical act of cutting, tearing, and gluing as childish. Additionally, working in a way that requires technical skills may help shift perceptions from the process as predominantly arts-based, potentially improving willingness to engage with the process. Taking these factors into consideration, the option of an online digital version is likely to be preferable to various clients.

However, for others technology can be overwhelming and challenging. Therefore, creating an online collage has the potential to engender anxiety and frustration, especially if the client is inexperienced at using the necessary tools. To negate this, a video tutorial on using the recommended tools is available for clients to watch, with guidance to practice in advance of an individual or group coaching session. Specifically developed for coaching with collage, this tutorial is a resource[2] for coaches interested in delivering the technique online.

Alternatively, these clients can use magazines rather than the curated digital image library. This method also suits individuals who prefer a traditional approach and want to retain the tactile experience of working with the resources while creating their collage.

DOI: 10.4324/9781003017028-17

In this scenario, best practice is for the coach to demonstrate aspects of the process, as happens when in person. Facilitating this requires the following equipment:

- an external camera, such as a webcam
- a flexible mounting arm for mobile phones or cameras

As video conferencing platforms such as Zoom have a function to share content from a second camera,[3] this equipment importantly ensures the client can not only hear but also see the instructions for stages one and two.

Whichever approach the client chooses, the imperative to establish a safe space for using a creative coaching technique remains. As this also supports engagement, coaches are advised to follow the guidance in Chapters 11 and 12.

The Digital Library

When working online, the onus of the CCT remains on unlocking unconscious thinking to access internal knowledge, wisdom, and information through images. Consequently, as sourcing a selection themselves would involve conscious awareness and an evaluative process, the coach provides clients with a digital library of specially curated images. These are never made available in advance of an individual or group session, which prevents clients from making assumptions concerning which images they will use. As the library is online, it is accessible to share via links within a video conferencing tool, such as Zoom or similar platforms.

Library Contents

While coaches can curate a library using copyright free images from websites[4], there is a ready-made version[2] available that answers the question, "How do I source images for my clients to make a digital collage online? How can I possibly choose images that cover all the aspects of life, not to mention my client's aspirations are different from mine?" (Mark, Coach).

The images in this digital library are carefully selected based on insight regarding the types most often used in classic coaching collages. In this context, 'type' refers to the potential of an image to convey psychological and emotional meaning, rather than a focus on the subject matter content. Consequently, the collection includes:

- photos that elicit metaphorical language
- archetypal symbols
- images offering contrasting interpretations
- a variety of patterns, shapes, and colours
- words and quotes
- imagery with a depth of detail or complexity
- varied genres, photographic styles, and artwork

A diverse range of demographics feature in classic collages and the people in the online library reflect this, while also minimising stereotypical images of individuals and groups. This collection is proven to elicit the same unconscious access, insights, emotions, understanding, and breakthroughs experienced with the offline version.

Digital Differences

Naturally, there is a difference between using magazines and coaching in person with the CCT compared to a digital media library and delivering online. With the former, clients have the option to manipulate their images tangibly, cutting, tearing, crumpling, or folding them to change or shift meaning. They still cut and paste with the latter, but there is no direct physical interaction with the materials. Instead, editing tools provide alternative ways to alter the images, for example, duplication, resizing, flipping, rotation, rounding corners, and cropping. While some people choose not to utilise these techniques, everyone repositions their images on the virtual canvas until satisfied it feels right. Therefore, each person engages in play. This activity effectively facilitates internal dialogue as an individual seeks to create meaning through editing, questioning, reflecting, evaluating, and reframing. Accordingly, clients experience the same cognitive creativity, with associated outcomes, as if making a classic coaching collage.

Once completed, the composition also acts as a baseline. Therefore, if clients choose to create another digital collage, they are discouraged from altering the previous one. Instead, in producing a new collage, they benefit from experiencing the entire process again. Being digital, clients access the same digital library, offering opportunities to reuse images from their original collage, potentially in a different way that reflects both their internal and external changes.

Case Study | On Transformation

Rosie's first collage was created in June 2020 during a coaching with collage workshop, delivered as part of an online retreat with a theme of 'Resilience.' Following the event, attendees were offered an opportunity for an individual coaching session to explore their collage in more depth. Rosie was one of the clients who chose to pursue this option. Focusing on one image, the following short excerpt is from her first coaching session.

ROSIE: The lady coming out of the water, I believe I feel a little bit fearful like, like I don't wish something along those lines. It just hurt me a little bit you know, and sometimes I wonder if she just represents me.

ANDRÉA: And in what way would she represent you?

ROSIE: I don't know if it's the mysteriousness or if it's sort of like a negative aspect. She could represent sometimes I feel scared about other people's intentions. Like now with this company. I think they want to take advantage of me, especially at these times where there might be a lot of learning designers looking for jobs. Or maybe it's jealousy or envy. I just feel like that particular corner represents that. So yeah, probably out of all the pictures, this is the one where I have more of that response.

ANDRÉA: And how does it feel to have this response to that image?

ROSIE: It makes me wonder like, on a rational level, it made me think why do I feel like that? Is it another person or is it me? I know that I do tend to be very hard on myself without realising, so maybe it is my inner critic. But it's not a bad thing at all, it's not like I feel like I don't want to see it. I do see the whole thing, and when I put this collage together the top was always about 'this is what I want to be' kind of thing. And the bottom might be things that are also part of me, but is the foundation. Because I cannot deny it if I am a perfectionist in recovery, and so I think it's part of who I am.

Figure 14.1 Rosie's digital collage created in May 2020.

Figure 14.2 Rosie's second digital collage created in September 2020.

Rosie chose to continue coaching with collage over a period of four months, using this time to explore each image, their connections and meaning in depth. In September 2020 she decided to create a second digital collage with a theme of career choice. To clearly demonstrate how one of Rosie's shifts is reflected through her use of an image, the focus remains on the woman coming out of the water.

ROSIE: I guess I see her like valiant, balanced, serene, observant, persistent and I wrote that she's coming out of water, waiting for the right time to come up. For some reason, water always means something fluid, usually more powerful than fire. At least that's how I think of water, like nothing can stop it. It could harm, but generally speaking, I don't think of water in that way. I like to calm myself down by taking baths, and I like swimming and walking around lakes. People don't think much of water, they waste it sometimes but really, it's a resource. I have been in a house destroyed by flooding, so I have seen the destruction water can cause when it's not managed properly. So, it's funny that something that gives me so much peace and is beautiful can also be mismanaged in a horrible way.

ANDRÉA: When you talk about water like that, does that resonate with you?

ROSIE: It's a good question because I've got a feeling that maybe one of the underlying issues in this job is I sometimes feel there has been some mismanagement, probably of myself. Maybe people were overstretched, with no time to manage properly. But also, perhaps I could manage things differently. Like with water, a person can feel desperate, or a person can feel serene. For me, when I started doing swimming, I trained myself to calm down because water sometimes scares me. I like water and can swim, but I don't feel a confident swimmer. So sometimes I have to calm down to be able to swim faster. That's what I've been thinking about me. Maybe I could manage things differently.

ANDRÉA: You talk about their mismanagement, and potentially you could have managed things differently. Are you aware of times you could have done things differently?

ROSIE: There has been so much going on, it's very difficult to unravel it, but I have questioned myself if I am making things more difficult for myself, maybe trying to do too much and then overcompensating…I didn't think about that before.

ANDRÉA: And what could you be overcompensating for?

ROSIE: I guess it could be because I am new, or in this particular place I am a bit more mature than my peers, or because I don't know things. Maybe I'm compensating because some aspects of the job are pretty complex. Maybe at the end of the day it's overcompensating for feeling like I am not up to the challenge or good enough. I guess it's one way to summarise it.

ANDRÉA: And how did that feel sharing that with me?

ROSIE: Well, I feel relaxed about it. But in school, I didn't say to myself, "I'm going to do this massive thing," I just did it, and people sometimes said, "Oh that looks really good," so it's my own expectations. When I want to do something great it doesn't happen, but when I just do the thing I have to do, it works better than I thought when I don't pressure myself. I guess when I put extra pressure on myself things don't work well.

ANDRÉA: And how might you change that?

[Holding the silence for Rosie]

ROSIE: I've been doing a bit more meditation, and I've been doing more walks just to reflect on what's happening because I think I need time to process it.

ANDRÉA: Okay. So how do you feel about the image overall?

ROSIE: It makes me feel free and happy. I find it liberating. I think there is a lot of desire there to feel differently. I also felt I kept the woman in the corner very tiny, and something I've been thinking about is when that woman is tiny, that's why she looks scary. When you expand her, she doesn't look scary at all. She looks more serene and feels more relaxing.

ANDRÉA: *Rosie*, you've said how she's less scary when she's larger, is more peaceful and serene, and you talked about water and what it means to you. In terms of that transition in size and position, does that resonate with you?

Rosie: Yes, it's made me think whether I inadvertently managed to keep myself small, and then why I chose to do that. In regards to my work, it has made me think that I don't want to rush into another job. Maybe I could explore what I can do, if I decide to do something for myself.

Like Trinity's experience with fireworks,[5] Rosie's embodied experience of water through a flooded house and swimming, served as an additional source of knowledge that informed her meaning-making and increased self-awareness. Using digital imagery, Rosie externalised her internal process of change by altering both the size and position of the woman coming out of the water. Her first collage served as a visual reference, enabling her to easily contrast and understand the change that she had experienced, as well as notice the constants. Rosie's transformation resulted from the ongoing coaching with her initial collage, her reflections, a-ha moments, and writing between sessions.

Working with Groups

Group Sizes

For the group coaching session to offer the best value, the recommended maximum number is 12 (18 with a co-coach). However, to ensure the coach feels confident, their experience in online facilitation should be taken into account when deciding the group size, especially since clients will be using virtual scissors and canvas via an image editing tool. Because group members have varied skills with technology, this aspect of the online version always necessitates the coach providing some clients with a degree of support.

Furthermore, the potential risks associated with working with the unconscious are the same as when coaching in person.[6] For this reason, when expecting more than 12 in the group, coaches are advised to utilise the support of a co-coach. This person's role is to provide practical, technical, and emotional assistance to the clients and lead-coach alike.

When deciding the group size, it is worth noting that having less participants increases opportunities for final collective reflection to take place verbally, whilst higher numbers increases the need to utilise the video conference's chat feature. Although, as reflective practice, the differences between verbal and written feedback are noticeable, they both offer the group significant value.

Breakout Rooms

The breakout room feature provided by video conferencing platforms is used for all three stages of the CCT. These rooms offer a confidential and safe space where participants first gather their images and then create the collage before sharing openly through personal storytelling. Allocating just three participants per room enhances this sense of safety, particularly for stage three of the process, while also ensuring everyone has a chance to be heard and contribute in a meaningful way. The number of groups should be such that the coach(s) can join each room successively to ensure clients understand the guidance and check if anyone needs technical support.

Collage Creation

Online groups are more likely to request coaching with digital images rather than magazines, the main reason being the convenience of the ready-made library, rather than each person having to source an individual collection of magazines. Occasionally, there may be a mix of methods in the group. However, timings orient towards creating and coaching with digital imagery, which, in the absence of physical gluing, requires less time. Clients are made aware of this difference from the outset to help inform their choice of online method. Additionally, as they receive the tutorial before the session, coaches should offer clients support and be prepared to receive technical questions from them in advance of the event.

Considerations When Coaching Creatively Online

Sourcing Magazines

If using the classic version online, to ensure the unconscious mind's exposure to a wide range of images, clients must obtain a broad selection of magazines. They need advice and sufficient time to gather this collection. To support them, the coach shares guidance on the recommended genres and possible sources.[7] Finding the suggested choice of magazines may prove challenging for clients, depending on their location. However, they may opt to create a digital collage instead or potentially print the digital image library immediately before their session to use in place of magazines. In these cases, to avoid clients' advanced image choice, the link is sent a few minutes before the appointed coaching time. Unsurprisingly, the choice to print is very rare.

The Online Environment

As coaches are not in the same physical space with their client, they cannot see how they interact with the resources or pick up on physiological responses as easily as if they were together. To counteract this difference in the environment, the coach employs alternative strategies to support their client. From a practical perspective, this involves periodically checking on the client's progress and engagement with the process and giving brief, unintrusive reminders of the cornerstone advice[8] at regular intervals during stages one and two. To remain attuned to a client's more nuanced reactions, coaches can intensify awareness of the client's language and tone.

Technological Experience and Confidence

When deciding whether to use the CCT online, personal confidence with technology is a significant consideration for the coach. Firstly, there is a baseline competence level needed to work with video conferencing tools and the image editing platform. Secondly, clients often require support with technical issues, and there is an expectation that the coach has the skills to support them with this, particularly concerning the collaging tools. While there is recognition that coaches are not IT experts, some degree of knowledge is especially beneficial if clients encounter issues in this area. Naturally, there will be times when the coach cannot help the client. In these situations, there are usually alternative solutions in the way of workarounds. However, coaches who feel less assured are advised not to use the CCT online until they feel confident and equipped with the necessary technical skills.

Collage Coaching Combinations

Although clients are not encouraged to create a magazine collage combined with images from the digital library, there are opportunities to alternate approaches over the coaching period. Examples of this include creating a classic collage online (or in person) with ongoing coaching sessions via a video conferencing platform. Clients may then decide to make any future collages using the digital image library. This combination is possible in any order or as a mix and match approach. Whatever the client's decision, the collage is always shared on-screen for storytelling during the immediate and subsequent coaching conversations.

Online Outcomes

Whether conducted in the same room with the client or via a digital platform, the CCT fundamentally remains an experiential and immersive creative coaching tool. As testimony to the power of images, regardless of the format, they retain the capacity to unlock unconscious thinking, give voice to what is hidden and unknown, and facilitate in-depth, meaningful dialogue that creates behavioural shifts for clients. When delivering online, because coaches follow the same three-stage process, clients also benefit from the outcomes associated with both cognitive and visual arts-based creativity. As nothing of the original approach's attributes is lost, coaches can be confident that whichever method is chosen by clients, their core outcomes remain the same as they move towards their goals.

Notes

1 The word 'classic' is used to denote the original version of the CCT delivered offline.
2 See Chapter 15 | Resources.
3 A search on how to use two cameras to share content online returns a wide selection of video tutorials to choose from.
4 Examples of websites where images are currently (2021) available free of charge for personal and commercial use include Unsplash and Pixabay.
5 See Chapter 10 | Part 1: Storytelling Through Collage (Client Reflections re Figure 9.2.1).
6 See Chapter 11 | Facilitating a Safe Space to use a Creative Coaching Technique.

7 While this guide was created specifically for clients and coaches based in the UK, a number of the suggestions are applicable regardless of location.
8 Coaches who attend training in the Collage Coaching Technique™ learn this and all aspects of the creative tool.

Bibliography

Watts, A. (2020). *A rich visual language | The Psychologist.* The Psychologist. https://thepsychologist. bps.org.uk/rich-visual-language

15 Resources

Most of the resources found in this chapter were created by the author and are therefore copyrighted material. However, they are available to support coaches and their clients when working with the Collage Coaching Technique™. Unless otherwise stated they are accessible from www.unglueyou.co.uk.

The following three guides are in the book, but for ease of use, can be downloaded from the website in PDF format for sharing with clients:

Guide to Sourcing Free and Low-Cost Magazines

Created initially for coaches based in the UK, several suggestions remain relevant for those living in other countries. Furthermore, any sources that are not applicable may inspire alternative ideas, and coaches are encouraged to be creative where they look for magazines. The guide serves a dual purpose. It provides advice to help coaches build a stock of magazines for use with individuals or groups. For clients, it assists them in sourcing a collection for their coaching session. With the latter, the coach sends the guide to their client in advance of coaching online when creating the classic collage.

Materials and Preparation Guidance

The information contained in the preparation document was designed with clients in mind, but functions as a resource for coaches. For clients, it is sent before their online session to ensure they have all the necessary materials ready, and the environment is conducive to coaching creatively. While not included in the guide, the covering email recommends they allow at least an hour after their session to process and reflect on their learning and decisions.

For coaches, the guidance acts as a checklist when preparing to coach with the Collage Coaching Technique™.

Making the Most of Your Collage

Specifically developed for clients, this resource enables them to be proactive in taking advantage of the long-term benefits inherent in their collage as a visual and tangible object. Clients are sent a copy with their follow up email after their coaching session. A hard copy can be shared if coaching in person.

DOI: 10.4324/9781003017028-18

Other resources available on the website are:

- The curated digital image library which includes the author's photography and images sourced from www.pixabay.com and www.unsplash.com. At the time of publishing, these websites offered free images and royalty free stock. Included with the digital library are the video tutorial mentioned in Chapter 14 and a comprehensive guide for clients on preparing for coaching online. (This resource is available for coaches who have completed the skills-based training.)
- The research conducted by Lana Baqaeen on 'Mindfulness in Art-Making for Employee Well-Being' was unpublished at the time of going to print. However, the visually engaging abstract is available and recommended reading.
- Collage coaching cards, which are mentioned in more detail after the guides.
- Information concerning the author's ICF accredited training, 'Collage as a Creative Coaching Tool.'

Guides

1 Guide to Sourcing Free or Low-Cost Magazines (in the UK)

To maximise the choice of images available, source 10–12 magazines from as wide a variety of genres as possible.

Recommended Genres

- Art/design/ creativity
- Business
- Entertainment
- Food
- Garden & Home
- Music
- Nature/ wildlife
- Photography
- Political
- Religion/ Spirituality
- Science
- Specialist
- Sport
- Technology
- Travel

Typical Free Sources Include

- Your own
- Family, friends, and colleagues
- Local supermarkets
- Street magazines e.g., Timeout/ Covent Garden guide
- City guides e.g., (if and where they can be picked up for free)
- Theatres, museums, and other places of interest
- Instagram, Twitter, and Facebook (people give their collections away)
- Online samples (these require your email address)
- Keep a look out generally as they can be found in unexpected places

For a Small Price

- The local library
- Charity shops

- Car boot sales
- **Do not** use newspapers or magazines with similar paper thickness as the paper is too thin.
- **Do** limit the number of specialised women's and men's fashion and health as the images aren't varied enough for coaching with collage purposes. One of each is enough for individual or group work.
- Please don't take ones provided for patients at clinical waiting rooms.

2   Materials and Preparation Guidance

For coaching online with the classic collage.

- **Glue**

Glue sticks are cleaner, easier, and quicker to use than liquid glue. I would recommend Pritt Stick because it allows for some repositioning. Furthermore, the glue is made from 97% natural ingredients, and the sticks are fully recyclable. In my experience those that cost less aren't usually as strong and tend to dry out when not used.

- **Scissors**

These are not essential as you can tear around images. However, I strongly suggest having a pair so that you have options to tear, cut or both.

- **A3 card – 160gsm**

A3 (297 x 420mm) card provides enough room to play with the images. If A3 size card is unavailable, stick two A4 sheets together. For durability card is preferable to paper. While you do not have to use white card, it is standard because when colour is relevant, it manifests through the images.

- **A selection of various magazines**

See the 'Guide to Sourcing Free and Low-Cost Magazines (in the UK).'

- **Music**

A specially curated playlist is available as a free resource at unglueyou.co.uk. This music is both relaxing and inspiring, creating the right atmosphere for working with the unconscious. While not recommended, if you prefer to choose your own, it should be without words and engender a state of rest.

- **Mindfulness exercise**

A pre-recorded mindfulness meditation is available as a free resource at unglueyou.co.uk.

- **A table**

This must be large enough for the paper size, magazines and additional room to place your collection of gathered images. To avoid getting glue on it, you can protect the surface.

- **Tissues**

Coaching with collage can be a profoundly moving and emotional process. The tissues mean you are ready should this be your experience.

- **A Bin**

For unused images. Where the facility is available, you are encouraged to recycle these with your paper.

If possible, choose a well-lit space with natural light. It is also essential that you are not disturbed during the process of creating your collage. Your phone should be turned off, or on silent with all notifications muted.

3 Making the Most of Your Collage

- If you haven't already, date the back of your collage with when you created it. Doing this enables you to use it as a baseline for reflection.
- Display your collage somewhere you'll see it regularly. If you can't, consider taking a photograph and using it as a screensaver on your phone, computer, or tablet.
  - Because images are emotive, your collage will continue to inspire, focus, and motivate you long after the workshop. Therefore, it's important that you see it regularly, preferably daily.
- Write down any keywords, phrases or feelings that come up for you as you reflect further on the collage. These are indicators of your current mindset, behaviours, and beliefs. They can help bring clarity to your choices about what to do AND what not to do as you create your future, ensuring you focus your energy and resources in a way that will support your intentions.
  - Naming it (a single word or phrase), journaling and creating affirmations are additional ways to use the written word with your collage.
- Remember that as an **outward expression of your inner beliefs,** your collage is a valuable resource. Therefore, be intentional about using it to remind you of your decisions regarding:
  - what you do and don't want
  - who you are
  - how you want to be

This will include your vision, aspirations, values, strengths, behaviours, blocks and decisions.

- If you meditate, you can use it as a visual focal point while contemplating a specific image, word or the overall collage.
- Continue to share the story and meaning of the images with people that you **trust**. Keep yourself psychologically safe by only sharing as much as you are comfortable with them knowing.
  - Because some of your images will be symbolic or metaphorical, alternative meanings will continue to emerge over time. Sharing it with others is one way to facilitate further exploration, insight, and self-awareness.
  - **NOTE:** Interpretation of images is subjective based on your life experiences, education, demographics, values, beliefs, culture etc. Therefore, if someone sees a different interpretation in your images, check if it resonates with you. Other views are helpful for reflection but not as a substitute for trusting your own insights.
- The recommendation is to create collages at regular intervals. Besides visually marking your progress, it supports your continued journey of increasing self-awareness, growing confidence, remaining focused, being intentional, and achieving your goals through personal transformation.

Collage Coaching Cards

Collage cards are a set of individual mini collages and images that coaches can use as an alternative to guiding clients through the process of creating a collage. Working with cards provides clients with the same empowering outcomes as creating a collage. Essentially accessing unconscious thinking, surfacing emotional drivers, using symbols and metaphors for meaning-making and storytelling as a pre-cursor to the coaching conversation.

As expected, there are differences compared to collage creation, including the lack of embodied cognition experienced directly through the art-making process. Nonetheless, even without direct engagement in the tactile act of creating a collage, clients benefit from the knowledge and processing of remembered physical actions or responses (Foglia & Wilson, 2013). Therefore, a card featuring someone falling could contribute to learning through embodiment.[1]

Without a collage, there is also an absence of relationships, patterns, and connections that create the holistic overview and micro-stories present in their narrative. However, if clients have worked with multiple image cards during one coaching session or over several, they can be viewed together, offering an opportunity to notice any emergent themes. Additionally, when working with groups, collating members' individual cards together is a way of collaborating to create the sense of a collage.

Unlike creating a collage, clients do not have a permanent, tangible object for continued exploration and reflection. However, as the images are not copyrighted, clients are encouraged to take a photograph for reference. The same applies in groups, including when their images are combined.

Applications

The set is highly versatile, suitable for individual or group work, applicable in all coaching areas, and any client theme. They provide a different method of utilising images in coaching, such as in the following circumstances:

- the available time or space is not enough to complete a collage using the CCT
  - ▶ this outcome is more likely when working within the constraints of an organisation
- working with large groups
  - ▶ as a sole facilitator
  - ▶ when time is limited
- a client is reticent to use an ABM or chooses not to create a collage
  - ▶ the cards allow clients to benefit from using images without the arts-based element
- exploring specific topics within a coaching programme
  - ▶ the set enables clients to clarify their thoughts concerning a particular subject or meaning attached to certain words
- when coaches are not ready or choose not to facilitate the collage process
  - ▶ using images can build confidence in coaches as, through practice, they develop the Clean Language and other conversation techniques.

Besides omitting points that relate specifically to creating a collage, when using the cards with clients, coaches follow the same guidelines and explorative conversation techniques as the CCT.

Note

1 See Chapter 8 | Part 1: Symbols and Metaphors for Meaning Making and Self-Awareness (Embodiment).

Bibliography

Foglia, L., & Wilson, R. A. (2013). Embodied cognition. *Wiley Interdisciplinary Reviews: Cognitive Science, 4*(3), 319–325. https://doi.org/10.1002/wcs.1226

Acknowledgements

During the writing process I created three collages. One of them features phrases that I deconstructed and remade to read, "How a baby is created, there are screams, took a village to bring it into the world." These words reflect the time, energy, joy, frustration, patience, tears, determination, and creativity that brought this book into being, while acknowledging that it would not have been possible by myself. I am blessed with a close and loving family, loyal friends, and supportive colleagues who have encouraged me throughout my collage journey and the nineteen months it took to write this book. Many others' prayers and wishes for an enjoyable experience and successful book inspired and motivated me along the way. Together, we are the village that brought the book to life.

While thanks go to everyone, I want to express my deepest gratitude to those most actively involved. Firstly, my husband Andrew, you named UnglueYou® and have tire-lessly been here for me every step as I pursue my vision, even though it has required so many sacrifices, especially with the book. I love you deeply. To our daughter Liandra, my friend, wise woman, and confidant, I would not have grown so much as I wrote if not for your willingness to be there, listen and guide.

A huge heartfelt thank you goes to all my clients. You trusted me with your stories, dreams, and challenges. It has been a privilege learning so much from you as I developed the Collage Coaching Technique™, knowledge now woven into the fabric of the book. To those who contributed client reflections and case studies, I am especially grateful. Most are anonymous, but in sharing honestly and openly, your experiences inform, teach, and will hopefully inspire others.

As part of my writing process, I sent finished chapters to my sister Melisa Mills, Michelle Drapeau, Gill McKay, and Kathryn Eade for review and feedback. I can hardly believe how generous you were with your time and expertise. This book is undoubtedly better for your editing, honest feedback, insights, and ideas.

It would be remiss of me not to mention the pioneers across varied disciplines whose work I integrate into my practice, learn from and reference in the book. While there are too many to name individually, I am grateful to each one, past and present for sharing their thoughts, theories, and research with the world. The artists and photographers, whose art-work features, offer their work without copyright. Thanks to their generosity, the book is a richer visual experience for readers. I am also grateful to my publishers for their patience every time I asked for an extension.

Ultimately, as a woman of deep spiritual faith, I thank my Father God for breathing into this book by singing through my voice and playing through my hands.

Index

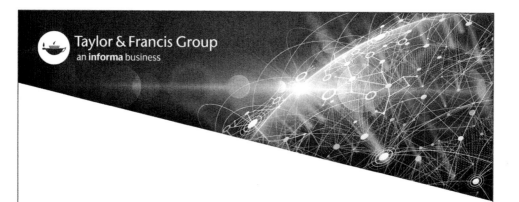

Printed in Great Britain
by Amazon

19144238R00099